THE LADDER:

Escaping from Plato's Cave

ANDREW MARKER

iUniverse, Inc.
Bloomington

The Ladder
Escaping From Plato's Cave

iUniverse books may be ordered through booksellers or by contacting:

*iUniverse
1663 Liberty Drive
Bloomington, IN 47403
www.iuniverse.com
1-800-Authors (1-800-288-4677)*

*Because of the dynamic nature of the Internet, any Web
addresses or links contained in this book may have changed
since publication and may no longer be valid. The views
expressed in this work are solely those of the author and do
not necessarily reflect the views of the publisher, and the
publisher hereby disclaims any responsibility for them.*

*ISBN: 978-1-4502-6434-1 (sc)
ISBN: 978-1-4502-6437-2 (ebook)*

Library of Congress Control Number: 2010915050

Printed in the United States of America

iUniverse rev. date: 12/06/2010

I do not think myself any further concerned for the success of what I have written, than as it is agreeable to truth.

—George Berkeley, *Principles of Human Knowledge*

Contents

Introduction

Imagine standing on the floor of a dark cave. A faint light emanates from the cave's mouth, high above your head. You want very much to get to the mouth, to see the light of day. So why not just go? The cave is not your prison. There are no shackles binding you to the bottom. You are free to move about as you please. Yet the walls of the cave are steep and slippery. You feel around in the dark but cannot find any footholds or fingerholds to help you up. Fortunately, lying on the cave floor, and right nearby, there is a ladder. You can climb your way out and make your escape!

Is the ladder long enough? There is no way to know for sure. Even if it is not, all is not necessarily lost. Perhaps the cave wall is broken by ledges you cannot yet see. If you could reach one of the lower ledges, you could pull the ladder up behind you and then use it to reach the next ledge higher up. This could be more work than you thought. You will have to put the ladder against the wall, climb up, and feel around for a ledge. If you cannot find one, you will have to climb down, move the ladder, and start over. Up, down, up again, over and over, moving rung to rung and ledge to ledge, until you reach the top. Even with all that effort, there is no guarantee it will work. Still, it seems worth a try.

Take the cave as an allegory. The cave represents our epistemic plight. The darkness represents the folly endemic to our species. The cave's depth symbolizes the depth of our natural ignorance. The daylight that enters the cave through the lofty mouth is the almost inaccessible light of wisdom. What of the ladder? That is the power of reason. We have to think our way to the top. Every clarified concept, every cogent argument, every exposed fallacy, every flash of philosophical insight, constitutes another rung on the ladder, another precious step towards the knowledge we desire.

The cave allegory is not original to me. Plato invented the allegory almost twenty-four hundred years ago, and it has been inspiring generations of philosophers ever since. Plato's *Republic*, where the allegory makes its appearance, was the first philosophy book I ever read, and it made me fall in love with philosophy. So I give Plato all the credit. It is still, and always will be, his cave. Yet my description of it differs from his: Plato never mentions any ladder. In his version, we are shackled within the cave. We spend our lives looking at shadows cast on the cave wall by the flickering light of a fire. Only some of us may be freed from our shackles. These lucky few find their freedom painful at first, but gradually, as their eyes adjust to the light, they come to see the cave more clearly. They can gaze at the fire and see the objects that were casting the shadows. Soon they can ascend the path leading out of the cave, where they meet the sunlit world. As their vision continues to improve, they advance step by step from one kind of object to another, until at last they may gaze upon the sun itself.

For Plato, the shadows—indeed, the whole interior of the cave—represented the transitory objects of the material world, the realm of coming to be and passing away. The sunlit world outside the cave stood for the realm of mind, containing the Platonic Forms, or Ideas, which are the eternal objects of philosophic contemplation. The sun was the ultimate Form, the Form of the Good. Plato thought that each soul gazed upon these Forms before birth, but then forgot what it had seen. Breaking the shackles involved "recollecting" what the Forms were like.[1]

I have always thought that Plato got the cave image exactly right. The image captures perfectly what it is like to be a philosopher. A philosopher is not a wise man. Rather, he is a fool who hates his folly enough to spend his life trying to escape from it. But those of us who place no faith in the Forms will very naturally experience life in the cave differently than Plato did. My retelling of the cave allegory describes how Plato's cave seems to me.

Plato inspired my general conception of philosophy, but it was William James who provoked my desire to write about the specific topics covered in this volume. I read James's *Pragmatism*, as well as his essay "The Will to Believe," while an undergraduate at St. John's College in Santa Fe, New Mexico, during the 1980s. I disagreed vehemently with much of what James had to say. I remember writing the word "no" next to countless paragraphs. Despite that, or rather because of it, James had a great influence on me. Authors whose views are congenial to us may be fun to read, but the authors who teach us the most are those whose views are the least congenial.

James postulated that on key religious issues, such as the existence of God, the evidence was inconclusive. The intellect could not be coerced into either believing or disbelieving. The will was therefore entitled to step into this epistemic vacuum and determine what to believe on faith. Such a position fit in neatly with James' pragmatic account of truth, which linked truth to utility. Scientific beliefs, James thought, are true because they are useful for explaining and organizing data, predicting phenomena, guiding research, and producing technological innovations. But he insisted that religious beliefs need not meet these scientific standards. They can be useful in other ways. They may promote morals, provide comfort, or add a spiritual dimension to life. If religious and scientific beliefs are equally useful, then, according to James, they are equally entitled to a place in our noetic structures.

I could not accept any of this. James' definition of truth seemed too anthropocentric. It showed no respect for the common-sense notion that there is a mind independent reality to which our beliefs ought to conform. James was correct in supposing that truths are often useful, and that sometimes their utility is a symptom of veracity. Yet many truths are not useful. Surely there are legions of truths totally unconnected to human purposes, and perhaps also truths permanently beyond the grasp of human investigators. Lies, on the other hand, are almost always useful to those who tell them. Why else do people lie? James' pragmatism offered no method for distinguishing between the truth and a universally convenient fiction. A cynic might say that was the whole point. Blurring that distinction justified James' permissiveness regarding religious belief. Still, as much as I objected to what James had to say, I had nothing of substance to put in its place. In philosophy, it is never enough to say "no." A naked "no" is obstinacy, not philosophy. To mean something, the "no" has to be backed up with reasons, and even then, there is an obligation to keep searching until a "yes" is found.[2]

The obvious alternative to James' pragmatism is the correspondence theory of truth. Alone among the more popular conceptions of truth, the correspondence theory has the merit of preserving the notion that truth involves a relation to reality. The correspondence theory holds that truth consists in saying that what is, is, and that what is not, is not. This is extremely plausible and, in fact, has been the dominant view in Western philosophy since ancient times. Yet it runs aground on one simple consideration: not all statements we are (pretheoretically) inclined to call "true" fit the model. We are not always trying to say what is or what is not. Sometimes we try to say what could be, should be, or would be. "Could," "should," and "would" statements are built into the fabric of our language. We could not remove them from our thoughts even if we wanted to. Are we to ban all such statements from the realm of truth, because they cannot be shoehorned into the correspondence mold? This would be unacceptably draconian. There has to be another way to fit reality into the picture.

The alternative I will present is called containment theory. Containment theory changes the model according to which truth is conceived. The correspondence model sees truths as corresponding to reality the way features of a map correspond to features of the mapped terrain. Containment theory, on the other hand, sees each truth as capturing reality within its domain. Reality is (one of) the fish caught in a true proposition's net. A fishnet-to-fish relation ties truth to reality somewhat more loosely than does the map-to-terrain relation. This slight loosening of the connection is what allows us to incorporate apparently disparate types of statements into the realm of truth.

Containment theory's objective is to preserve our common-sense notions of truth without burdening ourselves with metaphysical baggage, or prejudging the outcome of any philosophical debate. The "reality," for example, postulated by the theory, should be compatible with either a realist or an idealist view of what reality contains. I have already betrayed my bias in that area: I am a metaphysical realist. And part of the motivation for containment theory is to leave room for that kind of realism. Nonetheless, containment theory is constructed so as to allow equal opportunity for idealists, just in case I am wrong.

Containment theory achieves its objective by developing a theory of possible worlds. Exploiting the possible world concept to examine truth is not new. That concept's power, however, to solve the problems inherent in the correspondence model of truth, has not been widely appreciated. Containment theory will try to establish both the severity of those problems, and the elegance of a possible world based solution.

An examination of truth for different kinds of statements leads to the consideration of moral statements. This in turn leads back to issues of faith and God. Here, as with the question regarding truth, I will try to meet the challenge presented by James' outlook. I remain convinced that he erred in allowing the will to figure so prominently in the formation of belief. The will is not a reliable guide to truth. The will is intensely personal. Truth is impersonal. To respect truth, one has to respect its independence from our desires. When we do not have good reasons for belief, we cannot be content to believe whatever we are most motivated to believe. We have to continue the hunt for more convincing reasons.

I do not believe that there is a God, nor do I think reason impotent to decide the matter. Hence, I will try to construct a compelling argument to the effect that there isn't a God. My argument, which I call the argument from artifacts, is basically an attempt to hijack the classic design argument for the existence of God and turn it against theistic belief. The design argument was actually on the right track. We can and should be able to infer the existence or non-existence of God from the world's order. Where the design argument went wrong was in its estimate concerning the kind and quantity of order we can expect a divinely arranged world to display.

Although *The Ladder* pursues a single train of thought from beginning to end, its three essays are logically independent of one another. Each essay belongs to a different branch of philosophy. The first essay is primarily concerned with ethics. The second, which explains containment theory, falls within logic. The third essay defends the argument from artifacts, and so is a piece of theology, or metaphysics. One can accept or reject the conclusions of any essay, without committing oneself either way concerning the conclusions of the other two.

Those who wish to comment on any of the issues raised here may contact the author at cavesage@att. net. Readers are urged to consult the endnotes before offering comments. The endnotes address a number of technical details of the sort likely to give rise to objections.

Andrew Marker
September, 2010

First Essay:
What is Wisdom?

1

Philosophy is the most difficult subject. It is harder than rocket science or brain surgery. It contains more pitfalls than the most advanced branches of mathematics. Philosophers err more frequently than their peers in other disciplines, and they do a worse job of correcting their mistakes. Philosophers pursue more dead ends, take more wrong turns, and get lost more often than other scholars. When lost, they tend to stay lost, spending their whole careers stumbling through the dark. Ironically, the darker the intellectual terrain gets, the more confident a philosopher becomes of his own wisdom, and the more likely he is to see himself as a champion of truth and light. "What fools those other philosophers are!" he thinks. "If only they would listen to me, I could show them the way." Folly, over-confidence, and self-delusion are the philosopher's occupational hazards.

Philosophers as a group are not any less intelligent than other scholars, nor are they any more susceptible to human weaknesses. It is rather their subject matter that does them in. The sheer difficulty of philosophy at first seduces these lovers of wisdom, then spurs them to make heroic efforts, and then, in the end, spurns them.

2

What makes philosophy so hard? Consider this analogy with swimming. Many people know how to swim. Some of us are pretty good at it. However, none of us can swim as well as fish do. When it comes to swimming, any trout could put an Olympic-medal winner to shame. Human anatomy allows us to swim, but evolution did not design us to be swimmers. We are terrestrial creatures, with limbs and lungs built for use on land. In the water we are less efficient. Evolution also designed our brains. Unfortunately, it did not design us to be philosophers. It gave us big brains so we could make stone tools, plan hunting expeditions, woo mates, and outsmart rivals, not so we could explain the nature of justice, or define virtue. We mortals usually feel most at home when thinking about the ordinary, mundane, more-or-less concrete issues presented by daily life. Our brains also allow us to think about abstract theoretical issues, like those dealt with in philosophy, but since they are not built for that purpose, they are not very efficient at it. Were we creatures of pure intellect, perhaps we could philosophize as easily as fish swim.

But being embodied minds descended from apes, we find philosophy a struggle.

Science also deals with the abstract and theoretical. Yet it is still easier to do science than philosophy, because the scientist receives a form of help which the philosopher cannot get.

The whole world is at hand to help a scientist. Should he lose his way, the world will get him back on track by pointing out his mistakes to him. A chemist whose theory of molecules is faulty will soon know about it. The stuff in his test tube will turn blue instead of green. Rather than becoming cloudy, it will ignite. This is the world's way of telling the chemist he goofed. If an engineer has false beliefs, the world will be happy to disillusion him, too. The bridge he builds will collapse. The plane he has designed will crash. For a doctor who embraces an erroneous medical doctrine, the world performs a similar favor. It kills his patients. Scientists can always turn to the world for this kind of assistance. When their theories are off-base, the right experiments and observations will reveal this. In science, even the most abstract theory has to connect somehow to practical, concrete affairs. Each theory can thus be tested against how such affairs unfold. So while scientists make mistakes often enough, they do not persist in them indefinitely. They can discover their errors, learn from them, and move on.

To this extent, science is just like ordinary life. In our personal lives we know in due course when we get things wrong. Experience teaches us. The world does not suffer our errors in silence. It hits back. We take our lumps, learn from them, and move on. We are good at this kind of trial-and-error learning. Our brains are built for it. Our distant ancestors had to be able to learn in this same way. Early humans who had false beliefs about tigers were in trouble. If they did not modify those ideas quickly enough, they got eaten. Those who had a poor grasp of tool-making techniques went hungry. They discovered better techniques, or they starved. Our ancestors learned and moved on. If they could not learn, they did not become ancestors. Science, even at its most abstract, still presents us with something familiar—namely, a world where ideas have consequences, and where false beliefs betray themselves by their unpleasant fallout. We are comfortable in such a world, and well suited to meet its demands.

How differently things stand in philosophy! A philosopher who reasons badly about the nature of human consciousness will not lose consciousness because of that. A theologian whose idea of God is inadequate does not go straight to hell. No one dies because of their false beliefs concerning virtue, justice, or democracy. Platonists and Aristotelians, Humeans and Kantians—it rains on all alike. Determinists and Libertarians can both live long, happy lives, no matter who turns out to be right. The world is remarkably tolerant of false philosophies. Usually and for the most part, it does not hurt to be wrong.

But if the world does not hurt us for doing philosophy poorly, neither does it offer any help. The philosopher who looks to the world for answers to his questions will find that world mute. No laboratory experiment can settle the issue of free will. Field observations will not distinguish realism from idealism. Scientific data can reveal much about what is, nothing about what ought to be. Experience can teach us only within limits. Philosophy is what happens when we strive to get beyond those limits. Going beyond those limits, however, means that we go without help. Philosophers have to push forward using nothing but their own internal compasses, and these compasses are not designed for the task.

What about mathematics? Nothing is more abstract than mathematics, which, like philosophy, must advance without the aid of experiment and observation. Mathematicians also must rely entirely upon their own internal resources. Yet as difficult as mathematics can be, it is still not as hard as philosophy. A mathematician who ventures off into the realm beyond experience goes largely unencumbered. He takes his curiosity with him, but leaves most of his other passions behind. He normally has no personal stake in the outcome of his investigations. Whether $X = 5$, 12, or some other number, makes no difference to him. All that matters is that the right answer be found, and that it be proved with rigor. Should a mathematician allow vanity or ambition to cloud his judgment, his colleagues have ways of setting him straight. If his beloved proof turns out to be invalid, they can expose its fallacies with logical arguments even he must accept. Mathematics is remarkably impersonal this way. The joy of the subject lies precisely in this feature: it allows its practitioners to free themselves, at least temporarily, from their passions, prejudices, and idiosyncrasies, while they contemplate universal truths.

Philosophers do not travel so lightly. When they set off across the intellectual landscape their hopes and fears go with them. Their emotional needs, spiritual yearnings, and personal preferences become their baggage. Moreover, such things become the stars by which they navigate. Philosophers do have a personal stake in the outcome of their investigations. It matters a great deal, to them and to all of us, whether a material world exists, whether human beings have free will, and whether there is or is not a God. Philosophers, like mathematicians, strive to discover universal truths, and to achieve logical rigor in their arguments. But with so much extra baggage to carry, philosophers find the going much tougher. Passion clouds judgment much more often in philosophy than it does in mathematics, and dissipating the clouds is less easy. The philosopher is constantly at risk of allowing his prejudices and preconceptions to become lifelong blind spots. His colleagues will of course try to set him straight. But why should he listen to them? "Those ignorant fools don't know what they are talking about. How feeble their arguments are, compared to mine!" Or so the errant philosopher repeatedly tells himself until the day he dies.

This is why philosophy will always be the hardest subject. Philosophers seek wisdom. Unfortunately, wisdom is harder to find than knowledge. Factual knowledge may be acquired even by the denizens of Plato's cave. We can learn all kinds of interesting things about our cave, and when we get things wrong, the cave will let us know, with its own unique brand of aversion therapy (our planes crash, the tigers devour us, and so on). Attaining wisdom requires us to escape the cave, as Plato said. But where are the ladders to get us out?

And how do we avoid climbing imaginary ladders to a merely pretended wisdom?

3

We could begin by saying what wisdom is. Becoming wise may be difficult, but explaining what the word means ought not to be. If we knew our objective, if we knew what it was that we philosophers say we are seeking, then the task of climbing towards it might not seem so daunting. So, what is wisdom?

Wisdom is a property of persons. Plants, animals, and inanimate objects cannot be wise. Laws and institutions may be wise only in a derivative sense, to the extent that they embody the wisdom of their creators. In the primary sense, wisdom is reserved for rational beings, beings endowed with minds, beings capable of formulating concepts, articulating beliefs, and acting with forethought—in other words, people.

Some traits are prerequisites for wisdom, though not part of wisdom proper. Stupidity and ignorance preclude wisdom, as would gross moral failure. There is no such thing as a wise thief, rapist, or serial killer. It is not enough for the wise man to sit serenely, contemplating the mysteries of the universe. He should know a great deal about that universe, and be able to articulate his insights concerning it. Intelligence, sound moral character, and a good education—including a thorough acquaintance with history, literature, and the sciences—are all aspects of wisdom. One could possess those traits in abundance and still be a fool, yet one cannot be wise without them. They are the foundation upon which wisdom is built.

If moral virtue is not a part of wisdom proper, intellectual virtue is. Regrettably, the intellectual virtues receive scant attention. The discipline of intellectual ethics is nearly unheard of. Yet having a good mind is more than just being smart, articulate, and well educated. It also means cultivating certain desirable habits. What makes these habits so desirable is that they are all catalysts for clear thinking. Possessing such habits makes it less likely that a philosopher will stumble down the wrong path, blind himself, or climb imaginary ladders.

Chief among the intellectual virtues is curiosity. Curiosity is that insatiable thirst for knowledge that leads to a lifetime of intellectual endeavor. All the great philosophers had it. Socrates provided the original model and paradigm. He philosophized from youth into old age and kept up his inquiries until the day he died. Never content or complacent, he always strove to do better and know more. That is what it takes. One cannot retire from philosophy. The quest never ends.

One might say that curiosity is a matter of desire rather than habit; consequently, it cannot be a virtue. I beg to differ. The virtues are all about intellectual perception. But you will not see if you do not look. To be curious is to be in the habit of constantly, restlessly looking. It is not just a matter of desire. Instead, it is a matter of perpetually manifesting that desire through thought.

The second intellectual virtue is humility. Think of it as the Siamese twin of curiosity, for the two are inseparable and mutually indispensable. Why? Because you will not look for what you think you already have. If you believe yourself to be wise, you will cease the search for further insight. You may continue to expound and defend your views, but you will no longer see any need to improve them. Your curiosity will be dead. You will not even be a philosopher anymore, just a philosophical apologist—the difference being that a philosopher seeks new knowledge, while the apologist makes himself the keeper of a fossilized philosophy. To engage in philosophy is, at least tacitly, to admit ignorance. A restless, lifelong search for wisdom implies an acute awareness of one's foolishness. The philosopher keeps seeking what he knows he does not yet possess. Without humility philosophy comes to a halt, because the curiosity that drives it dies. Yet, without curiosity, humility has no merit. It is either a craven submission to ignorance, or a pledge of allegiance to dogma.

An old joke claims that when a PhD gets his doctorate, he becomes incapable of saying two things: "I don't know," and "I was wrong." An ability to say the first indicates humility. An ability to say the second suggests another virtue—the virtue of being open-minded. Open-mindedness has two aspects. The first is the ability to be convinced by an opponent's arguments (when they are cogent), or by his criticisms (when they are telling). Ever since Plato, philosophy has consisted of conversations. We might think of the whole philosophical community as having spent the last two millennia engaged in one long conversation, a seminar or symposium in which arguments and counter-arguments get traded. This conversation would be so much wasted breath if even cogent arguments could never have any impact. Being open to persuasion is thus the price of admission to this grand debate. People with doctorates do not really lack this quality, by the way. Only trial lawyers do. Imagine a lawyer standing up in the middle of a trial and admitting that his opponent's arguments had convinced him. "Well, I'll be!" he might say. "It turns out my client is guilty after all. The evidence is irrefutable!" This hardly ever happens.

The second aspect of open-mindedness is much rarer than the first. It involves not just passively waiting for others to point out your errors to you, but actively looking for such errors. Obviously you don't know which of your beliefs are false. If you did, they would not continue to be your beliefs. Still, you know there must be some falsehoods mixed in with your beloved truths, and you want to keep weeding these out—intellectual gardening, if you will. As Nietzsche suggested, the important thing is not to have the courage of one's convictions, but to have the courage for an attack on one's convictions.[3] Both aspects of open-mindedness presuppose a high degree of humility. A vain mind closes quickly.

There is another virtue, related to open-mindedness, called charitableness. It consists of applying the principle of charity to statements made by others, especially including the statements of one's intellectual opponents. According to the principle of charity, a statement ought to be interpreted in whatever way makes the most sense of it. The charitable interpretation is the one that makes the speaker appear the most reasonable, the one that attributes to the speaker the greatest possible degree of common sense and intelligence. The charitable person does not have to believe that his fellow men are all paragons of rationality. Many of them are probably morons. As for his intellectual opponents, they must be fools. Why else would they have become his opponents? But the charitable person still tries to put his opponents' views in the best possible light, not the worst. He wants his opponents to have insights so he can learn something from his conversation with them. He therefore strives to draw as much wisdom out of their remarks as he can. If he accidentally draws out more insight than was actually in them, fine. His opponents will not mind being thought wiser than they are, and everyone can still benefit from those extra insights. By contrast, the uncharitable person would prefer his opponents say stupid things so that he can expose their stupidity and win the argument. He therefore pretends that his opponents have less insight than they do. He attributes absurd opinions to them. What he ends up refuting are not the real arguments of his flesh and blood opponents, but the caricatured arguments of imaginary "straw man" opponents. This is both a waste of his time and a source of frustration for his victims. Clearly some charity is needed to keep the wheels of philosophical conversation engaged.

Before taking up the next intellectual virtue, I want to pass on to the reader a parable I encountered many years ago. I do not remember where I found this story. What I read was not a primary source, but the nth generation reworking of a tale that had been told and retold countless times. The oral tradition from which the story emerged could go back centuries. My account will differ from previous versions. I cannot quote word for word, but must paraphrase based on decades-old memories. Given that the material resides in the public domain, I may therefore be permitted the liberty of modifying the parable to suit my purposes:

One day a young man went to the Master and said, "Master, I wish to learn Kung Fu."

"Oh do you?" the Master replied. "Well, is not that interesting! Sit down right here." The young man sat where the Master had pointed, while the Master took a seat across the table, facing his new student. "Take this teapot, would you?" the Master said.

"Whatever for?" asked the student.

"I want you to pour me some tea, of course," said the Master. "Pour it into this cup I hold in my hand."

The young man tried to do as his Master requested but found the task impossible—since the Master held the cup way overhead, where the young man could not reach it. "I cannot do as you say," the young man complained. "You have placed the cup too high."

"Very well," responded the Master. "I will lower the cup." The cup was indeed lowered. In fact, it rested right on the surface of the table. But now the Master kept his hand over the cup, so again the student was frustrated.

"I cannot pour the tea when you cover the mouth of the cup," he said. "Please remove your hand."

"Certainly," said the Master, whereupon he turned the cup upside down and placed his hands in his pockets.

"That is no better," complained the student.

Finally the Master placed the cup in the proper position, and the young man poured the tea. As it turned out, however, the cup contained a hole, so the tea spilled onto the table and even trickled down to the floor. "What is the meaning of this, Master?" asked the student. "What are you trying to tell me?"

"The first cup, the one I held overhead, symbolizes the arrogant pupil," replied the Master. "The arrogant pupil puts himself above his teacher because he thinks himself smarter than the teacher. Hence, he learns nothing. He puts himself so high that knowledge cannot reach him.

"The second cup, which I covered with my hand, symbolizes the stubborn pupil. He refuses to accept anything he is told because, to his narrow little mind, it all seems so implausible. 'That cannot possibly work!' he keeps telling himself. Therefore, he never realizes that what seems crazy at first will make sense later, if an effort is made to find the sense.

"The third, overturned cup symbolizes the apathetic pupil. He learns nothing because he does not want to learn anything, and because paying attention would be too much work.

"The fourth cup symbolizes the pupil who listens carefully, yet does not hear; who watches with both eyes wide open, yet sees nothing. He fails to understand what he is taught, and what he does understand, he soon forgets. He can parrot his teacher's words, he can mimic his teacher's actions, but the meaning of the words, together with the purpose of the actions, is lost on him. Hence, he is like the cup with the hole in it, the cup that received all the tea that was poured into it, only to spill its tea immediately onto the table.

"So do not be like any of these cups. Be like this one." With that the Master stopped speaking. He picked up another cup, one without holes in it, and held it in front of him, toward the young man. The young man had no trouble pouring tea into this fifth cup, nor did any of the tea spill out."

The parable illustrates the virtues I have discussed. A humble mind is like the cup that one has placed on the surface of a table. By keeping its ego in check, it puts itself on a plane where learning can occur. An open mind is like a cup that no hand covers over. Knowledge can flow in because the entrance to the mind is not damned shut. As for the cup turned right-side up, that is like the curious mind that wants to turn itself toward every available source of information. And the cup without holes resembles the charitable mind. The charitable mind retains the insights offered by rivals because it recognizes their value.

As it stands, however, the parable appears to discourage independence of thought. Why risk thinking for ourselves? If our master has all the answers, we need only listen to him, understand what he says, and believe. Critical reflection is unnecessary. The master (or his master, or his master's master …) has already taken care of that. There is no need to correct the master's mistakes. He has not made any. The master's tea is entirely wholesome. We simply hold out our cup, receive the tea he pours us, and drink.

Unfortunately, in the real world things are not so easy. We cannot afford to be so passive. Real masters are fallible human beings. They have blind spots, unexamined prejudices, and false beliefs. Sometimes their tea is not wholesome.

The traditional story ended with tea being poured into the fifth cup. But suppose we take this conformist's parable and transform it into a parable for free thinkers. All we have to do is add a sixth cup:

Years went by as the young man trained daily, learning as much Kung Fu as the Master would teach. Then one day the Master called upon his student to sit with him once again at the table where tea was served. After they were seated, the Master asked his student to pour him some tea. The young man tried, but the Master held the cup too high, just as he had done on the day they met. The young man guessed what his Master was up to, so he played along, and the two of them went through the whole sequence of five cups, step for step and word-for-word, exactly as they had during that first meeting. But this time, when the young man had finished pouring tea into the fifth cup, the Master simply dumped the tea into a nearby flowerbed. He then grabbed the teapot out of his student's hands and smashed it against a tree. Having done so, he once again held out his cup.

"What do you want?" asked the student.

"I want you to pour me some tea," replied the Master.

"The tea is all gone," said the student.

"So brew some."

"But how?" the student asked.

"Must I do everything for you?" the Master snapped. "Just figure it out."

The young man was stunned at first, but presently he got up and left the room. He came back a short while later with a fresh pot of tea, some of which he poured into his Master's cup.

"Congratulations," said the Master. "You don't need my tea any more. You have learned to brew your own. You don't need my Kung Fu any more either. What you don't yet know, either I cannot teach to you, or you could discover better on your own. So go, get out of here. You are a student no longer, but a master in your own right."

The young man left the room once again, but this time he never came back.

Every aspiring philosopher begins his studies with access to unimaginable wealth. He has at his disposal, not the wisdom of just one Master, but that of many. Each and every one of the great philosophers can be his "Master," for he has an opportunity to learn from all of them. Plato, Aristotle, Aquinas, Spinoza, Hume, Kant, and Wittgenstein are all members of the faculty from which he can take instruction. But if he does no more than learn what those great thinkers said, then he is no philosopher. At best, he is an historian of philosophy. To be a philosopher is to be an independent thinker, learning, of course, from the insights of others, but also recognizing their mistakes and then fashioning from the rubble of their failed theories a philosophy uniquely his own. At some point a philosopher learns to brew his own tea, in a pot of his own making, using leaves from his own garden.

The ultimate virtue on our list is thus the virtue of independence. Independence presupposes all the prior virtues. Without them, it is no virtue at all, but mere rebelliousness and antipathy towards authority. Independence also provides a counterweight to the others. One must be humble, but not so humble as to lose self-confidence. One ought to be charitable, but also critical. The independent mind has to find the right balance among these things. What it seeks is not simply to be different, but to be free—free from subservience to any one master, free from whatever errors previous masters might have promulgated, free from their biases, prejudices, and presumptions.

Here again, one might question whether independence is a habit. Think of a fly placed inside a screened-in porch. The fly will crawl around on the screen until it finds a way out. If there is a hole in the screen the fly will find it, even if the hole is very tiny, and even if the porch is very large. The independent mind is like the fly. Whatever intellectual trap it is in, whatever box its masters have placed it in, it will find a way out. It just keeps probing until it tumbles through a hole and makes its escape into the open air. Even if there are boxes inside screens inside boxes, the independent mind never stops. Independence is this recurring pattern of intellectual behavior, and such patterns are precisely what we refer to when we speak of mental habits.

But what if one's master has not erred? What if there are no holes in his screen? Even then, one still has to look. The only way to know that there are no holes is to make a thorough search for them. One should not poke holes where there are none, nor pretend to escape through imaginary holes. One will merely search doggedly for real holes. There is still virtue in the search, even if there turn out to be no holes. Socrates claimed that the unexamined life is not worth living. We might add that the unexamined philosophy is not worth having. The adherent to an unexamined philosophy would not count as wise, even if that philosophy represented the final truth about things. His "wisdom" would result from luck—he was lucky enough to have a good master— rather than skill. Skill at philosophical inquiry is even more important than knowledge. A skillful philosopher will find the answers in due time, while a philosopher with all the answers may never gain the skills necessary to acquire answers. Besides, there are always holes.

To the elements of wisdom already discussed— intelligence, general knowledge, good moral character, and intellectual virtue—only one more needs to be added. This is philosophical knowledge, which consists in "knowing all the right answers" to philosophical questions. One cannot be wise and also mistaken about important philosophical issues. The wise person has to get these matters right, he has to be right for the right reasons, and he has to be able to explain and defend his views in a rational manner. The person who has all that covered is wise. He has reached the top of the ladder.

With respect to the earlier criteria for wisdom, we can tell if someone meets them. Intelligent and well-educated people are easy to spot. Scoundrels always betray themselves eventually, and if someone is closed-minded or uncharitable, that will come out in conversation, or by reading what they have written. Recognizing that someone "knows all the right answers" is a knottier matter. To know that they know the right answers, one would have to know the right answers. One has to be wise to spot a wise person. But how could we possibly know that we ourselves are wise? Can we measure our own wisdom? Surely wise people ought to know that they are wise. However, for every truly wise person, there must be thousands of pretenders. How does a wise person know that he is not one of the pretenders? The odds would appear to be against him. Possibly the wise person does not know. Perhaps this is one area where knowledge is impossible, and one must be content with true belief. Wise people believe, correctly, that they are wise, and they can spot others who are. But they do not know. If they think they know, then they are not really wise. The possibility always remains that one's screen has undiscovered holes. Did I mention that philosophy is hard?

The reader may think that I am making philosophy sound harder than it is by making the conditions of knowledge too strict. "Of course the sage knows that he is wise," the reader might retort. "We define knowledge as 'justified true belief,' where the believer is in the right cognitive position to make an accurate judgment. The sage believes he is wise. His belief is both true and justified. He can explain why his philosophical views are correct. He holds those views for the right reasons, so he has good grounds for thinking himself wise. He is also in the right cognitive position to make an accurate judgment in this matter. Since he is wise, he can tell who is wise, and this includes being able to tell that he himself is wise."

I would accept the definition of knowledge given, while adding one further condition. A belief counts as knowledge only if it is held with some confidence; the confidence, as well as the belief, being justified. If the believer is hesitant and unsure, if his belief comes attended with much doubt, then he cannot be said to know. If he does not doubt, but ought to, then again his belief is not knowledge. Adding this extra clause does not make our definition too strict. On the contrary, it is necessary to bring the definition into conformity with ordinary usage. We would not claim to "know" something unless we felt sure. Absolute certainty is not required, but considerable and well-grounded confidence is.

Such confidence is never justified when one claims to be wise. The error rate is too high, the probability of being right is too low, for the claim to ever amount to knowledge. So again, the sage may believe, but he can never know, that he is wise. And even when he does think himself wise, he will continue to act on the contrary assumption. He will continue the search for holes.

Second Essay:
What is Truth?

1

The wise person, or sage, knows the answers to philosophy's problems. The answers consist of truths about the world, about our place in it, about the nature of rationality, and so on. What, then, is truth? We were able to say what wisdom is without being wise and without having to identify anybody who was. We had only to identify a concept. We unpacked a piece of our own mental luggage. Perhaps, in a similar fashion, we can say what truth is without knowing all truths, or even any truths. We just need to do some more unpacking.

We may call this question about truth Pilate's question. Recall the passage in John where Pilate says to Jesus:

> "Your own people and chief priests handed you over to me. What is it you have done?"

Jesus said, "My kingdom is not of this world. If it were, my servants would fight to prevent my arrest by the Jewish leaders. But now my kingdom is from another place."

"So you are a king, then!" said Pilate.

Jesus answered, "You say that I am a king. In fact, the reason I was born and came into the world is to testify to the truth. Everyone on the side of truth listens to me."

"What is truth?" retorted Pilate. (John 18:35-38, Today's New International Version)

Pilate puts a very Socratic question to Jesus. He asks what truth is. One thinks of Plato's dialogue *Meno*, in which Socrates asks Meno to tell him what virtue is, and also of the *Euthyphro*, in which the same type of question arises regarding piety. Jesus' very un-Socratic answer is given four chapters earlier. There, in John 14:6, Jesus claims to be the truth: "I am the way and the truth and the life." The trouble is, even if Jesus were both the way and the life, he still could not be the truth. Jesus' comment about truth makes inspiring rhetoric, but poor philosophy.

Imagine Jesus talking to Socrates. Socrates asks what truth is, and Jesus responds by announcing that he, Jesus, is the truth. Readers of Plato know what Socrates would say: "No, no, Jesus, that is not the kind of answer I had in mind. What I want to know is, what do all truths have in common? What is it that makes them all truths?" And Socrates would be right. Defining truth does not mean giving a fine speech about it. A definition of truth cannot be a list of truths either. The list would go on forever. Least of all can the definition involve pointing to or naming a person. Even if the person named or pointed to were omniscient, we still would not have what we were looking for. A definition of truth must say what all truths have in common. It should find the underlying unity in the class of truths.

So Jesus' answer to Pilate's question will not do. Arriving at a better answer, however, presents problems. The set of truths is heterogeneous. The sentences we feel inclined to call "true" display different logical structures. They do different jobs in our language, serve different purposes, and have different kinds of meanings. It is not obvious what the underlying unity of all those sentences might be. Consider these examples:

1. William, Duke of Normandy, defeated King Harold of England at the Battle of Hastings in 1066.
2. An object in motion tends to stay in motion, and an object at rest tends to stay at rest, unless acted on by a force.
3. $2 + 2 = 4$
4. It is morally wrong to commit rape.

The first sentence, S(1), makes a statement about a matter of historical fact. It tells us what happened during the eleventh century. S(1) has a logical form something like "X is the case," or "This is how the world is," where "is" has no tense.

The second sentence, S(2), is Newton's first law of motion. It too states a fact about the world, albeit one far more general than that related in S(1). S(1) refers to a single, epic event, an event narrowly confined in space and time. The Battle of Hastings transpired in a day and was fought on a field only a few hundred yards across. By contrast, S(2) concerns a class of events broad enough to include the actions of every physical object that ever has or ever will exist. But to say that S(1) represents a particular, and S(2) a universal, understates the matter. S(2) also represents what would happen in a potentially infinite variety of hypothetical situations. According to Newton's Law, any given moving object (which was once at rest) would have remained at rest, had no force moved it. Any given stationary object (which had been moving) would have remained in motion, had some force not stopped it. Therefore, S(2) pertains to both what does happen and to what would happen. Its logical form is not "X is the case," but more like "X both is the case, and would be the case, under various unrealized circumstances."

Now consider the next sentence, S(3). What logical form does it have? At first, S(3) looks as though it might fit the model of S(2) because it states a universal fact. It really is the case that every quartet of objects consists of two pairs. Find any two pairs of apples and put them together: the result is a collection of four apples. Like S(2), S(3) covers hypothetical cases. Two apples, combined with two more, would make four apples, under all imaginable circumstances, including an infinite variety of circumstances never to be realized.

However, there is still a big difference between S(3) and S(2). S(2) states a logically contingent fact, S(3) a logically necessary one. The truth of S(2) depends on the existence of a material world where objects behave in a specific way. If there were no material objects, or if material objects behaved differently, then S(2) would be false. We can imagine a world free of material objects, a world, for example, that was nothing but empty space. We can also imagine worlds where objects spontaneously start and stop without any external forces acting upon them. We can thus imagine S(2) to be false. We cannot do this with regard to S(3). Let your imagination run wild, conceive of any world you please, and two plus two in that world will still equal four. Every quartet will consist of two pairs. Even in a world composed only of empty space, two plus two would equal four. There could be four points, four lines, and so on. But what if we remove the space, so that the world contained absolutely nothing? It would make no difference. Two plus two would still be four, because S(3) is a matter of logical necessity. Its truth does not depend on the world being any particular way.

S(2) says something about the world. It presupposes that there are material objects and then describes both how those objects actually behave and also how they would behave under various circumstances. S(3) says nothing about the world. It does not tell us what is the case. There does not have to be anything the case, in order for S(3) to be true. S(3) makes no assumptions regarding the world's contents. It merely says that if the world does contain things (points, lines, apples, or whatever), then those things aggregate in a certain way (two pairs combined always aggregate into a quartet).

So S(3) does not fit the model provided by S(2) after all. They have different logical forms. We might rephrase the form of S(2) thus: "X is the case in all realized situations, and X would remain the case in all realizable scenarios." For S(3), the form is closer to this: "If Y is the case, then Z is the case." If there are two pairs, then there is a quartet. This form allows S(3) to stay agnostic about whether or not the world contains any pairs. Y does not have to be the case in order for S(3) to be true. No such agnosticism is found in S(2).

Finally, look at S(4). S(4) is not about how the world is or would be. It is about how the world ought to be. It is equivalent to saying that men ought to refrain from raping women. S(4)'s logical form is thus "X ought to be the case." S(4) can have this form without actually employing the word "ought." What logical form a sentence has depends on the nature of the claim being made, not on its wording or grammatical structure.

The four sentences discussed represent a sampling of the types of sentences we typically call either true or false. Sentences like these are believed to have truth values. For the purposes of illustration, I naturally chose four sentences I am confident are true. However, the point they illustrate would remain valid even if all four were false. And the point is that truths display disparate logical forms.

But so what? So what if some truths concern what is, while others have to do with what would be, or could be, or should be? Why should any of that be a problem? Yet there is a problem. Our objective is to define truth by revealing truth's unity. This would be easier if all sentences possessing truth values had the same logical form. Unity of logical form would serve to bind the class of truths together. All we would have to do then is establish criteria for separating true sentences from false ones. Unfortunately, the unity of logical form we desire does not exist. How, then, can our Socratic project of truth definition even get started?

Perhaps we could reduce all the logical forms down to one super form. This would involve showing how sentences of any form could be translated into sentences having the super form. In every case the original sentence and its translation would have to be equivalent. Each sentence would have to entail the other. Unfortunately, accomplishing such a reduction is impossible.

To understand why, we need to draw on the insights of David Hume. Hume saw very clearly that there are logical chasms between sentences of different types. He knew, for example, that "is" never implies "ought." No statement or set of statements regarding what is the case ever logically entails that anything ought to be the case. No matter how the world happens to be, we are always free to suppose that it ought to be different. Questions concerning how the world ought to be cannot be answered simply by gathering facts. The facts do not tell us how to judge them. They cannot compel us to judge one state of affairs to be better than another. The chasm between "is" and "ought" gets bridged neither with facts nor with logic, but only by choosing to value one thing more than another.[4]

If "is" never implies "ought," then, by the same token, "ought" never implies "is." From statements regarding what ought to be, nothing whatsoever follows concerning what actually is. Consequently, we can never reduce "is" to "ought," or "ought" to "is." Sentences like S(4) can never be translated without remainder into sentences like S(1). S(1) and its logical kin are never precisely equivalent to moral judgments such as S(4).

The forms exhibited by these sentences are irreducibly different.

Well, one might say, so much the worse for moral judgments. If moral judgments do not fit the model provided by other truths, perhaps we should put them under quarantine, or even banish them from the realm of truth. This tactic, though favored by many, seems a desperate maneuver. Again, we have to stay focused on our goal, which is to unpack our ordinary, common-sense concept of truth. That concept does allow room for moral truths. Most of us believe in moral truths, unless philosophical reflection erodes our faith. We do not want to unpack our concept and then discover belatedly that we have thrown away the best suits in the case. Besides, banishing moral judgments from the realm of truth would only rescue us from one chasm. There are other chasms, equally great, which we have not yet addressed. There is, for example, a chasm between "is" and "would." Once again, our inspiration comes from Hume.

As Hume noted, the fact that events have always obeyed a certain law in the past provides no guarantee that they will obey it in the future. No matter how many times a law has been previously confirmed, the very next sequence of events might still flout it. Of course, we generally do assume that, in some sense, the future will mirror the past, and that the patterns, laws, or regularities we have observed so far will continue to display themselves henceforth. Basing expectations upon experience is not only rational, it is an essential part of what it means to be "rational." However, no statement or set of statements about the past actually entails the truth of any statement or set of statements about the future. From the premise "The sun has risen every day for billions of years," the conclusion "It will rise tomorrow" does not follow. No matter how strong we might think the evidence for the latter proposition to be, it is still possible to conceive its falsehood.[5]

What Hume discovered might be called the chasm between "was" and "will be." Statements about the past and present do not entail, and are not equivalent to, any statements about the future. The future cannot be reduced to the past or present.

The chasm between "is" and "would" is formally identical to that between "was" and "will be." It exists for exactly the same reasons. Hume would have loved it, and without his help I would not have seen it.

If nature exhibits a given regularity in all actual events, past, present, and future, there is no guarantee that it would exhibit the same regularity in all, or any, contra-factual cases. It always remains possible that the regularity would fail in one or more hypothetical situations never to be realized. That a given regularity pertained to all actual events would constitute overwhelming evidence for the thesis that it was indeed a law of nature, valid for all relevant contra-factual scenarios. We believe, rationally, that the sun would have risen the day after the Battle of Hastings, even if Harold had emerged victorious. However, the opposite supposition, though seemingly preposterous, is not literally inconceivable. The evidence may be overwhelming, but it does not amount to proof. "Is" does not imply "would," any more than it implies "ought" or "will be."

The desired reduction of "would" statements to "is" statements is thus impossible. In this case it is not even plausible to banish the offending statements from the realm of truth. Abstaining from contra-factual beliefs is not one of our options. We could not get through a single day without beliefs of that type. To make rational choices in life, we have to know what the probable consequences of possible actions would be. We have to know what would happen if we took this course of action, what would happen if we took that course, and so on. Knowledge in this area is necessary and, therefore, possible. As a plain matter of fact, we frequently do know plenty concerning what would, or would not, be the case. What is it that we know, if not truths?

Similarly, we cannot banish mathematics from the realm of truth. The truths of arithmetic and geometry are among our paradigms. Without them the concept of truth would melt away. Yet we cannot reduce mathematics to anything else. We cannot, for example, treat arithmetic statements as if they were laws of nature. That approach might work well enough for S(3)—"it is a law of nature that two apples, combined with two more, always equals four apples, and so generally, for pears, oranges, and any other type of object"—but the approach breaks down when we think about imaginary numbers. Make a pile of apples containing two times the square root of negative-one apples. Now combine it with another pile of similar size. What result do you get? Mathematicians have an equation for this:

$$S(3)' \quad 2\sqrt{-1} + 2\sqrt{-1} = 4\sqrt{-1}$$

Most of us would be inclined to call this equation a mathematical truth. Is it a law of nature? One wonders what part of nature that would be. It cannot be the part with apples in it.

2

This irreducible variety among truths creates an insurmountable difficulty for the correspondence theory of truth. The correspondence theory maintains that truth consists in saying that what is, is, and that what is not, is not.[6] The correspondence theory does an admirable job of capturing our common-sense belief that truth must connect with reality. Correspondence model truth is just whatever bears the appropriate relation to the world "out there." This core idea is perfectly valid. Yet as we have seen, not all true sentences have the logical form of "X is (or is not) the case." So the truth-to-world relation upon which the correspondence model focuses cannot be the right one. For the correspondence theory, this is fatal.

The correspondence theorist can easily paper over the variety among truths. All he has to do is rephrase every true sentence by adding the phrase "it is the case that." "It is the case that William conquered England," "It is the case that material objects obey Newton's laws," "It is the case that two plus two equals four," "It is the case that men ought not to rape women." All truths thus adhere to a single formula. Unfortunately, forcing them into that form generates merely a verbal similarity among truths, leaving the logical differences among them untouched. Their resemblance is thus superficial and does nothing to solve the problem at hand.

The correspondence theorist could employ the phrase "it is a fact that." He could then make the claim that all truths state facts. That would be their underlying unity. He would actually be on to something here, since all truths do state facts. Yet even this tactic does not solve our problem. We are still faced with an apparently irreducible variety among facts. If the class of truths perplexes us so that we feel unsure as to what binds the class together, then the class of facts ought to perplex us just as much, for the same reason. "What," we might ask, "are facts? What common ground is there among historical facts, scientific facts, mathematical facts, and moral facts?" The correspondence theorist has done nothing to reduce our perplexity. He has only shifted it from one thing to another.

To resolve this conundrum, the correspondence theorist would have to say what all these different kinds of facts correspond to. If truth is a matter of correspondence and if all truths relate facts, then facts must correspond to something. To what do they correspond? There does not appear to be anything to which the fact related by S(3)′ might correspond. S(2)'s fact does not seem to correspond to anything either. S(2)'s fact covers contra-factual scenarios as well as actual events, but those contra-factual scenarios are never going to happen. So a portion of what S(2) claims to be the case goes beyond reality. Reality is just not big enough to underwrite that claim. And where exactly do we find moral facts? Ordinary historical facts we find easily enough. But between those and the moral facts lies Hume's chasm. In crossing that chasm, we go beyond what reality provides.

The correspondence theorist might try to salvage his theory by adopting some metaphysical presumptions. For example, he might claim that mathematical facts are underwritten by the Platonic Ideas of Number and Figure, while moral facts correspond to the moral edicts decreed by God. And what about contra-factual facts that deal with what would or would not occur? Those facts, he might say, refer to the inner essences of things. What a thing would or would not do depends entirely on its essence, or nature. If a thing has a certain nature, then it will of course act according to that nature under any and all circumstances that might arise. The existence of this nature, or essence, acts as the guarantor of any true contra-factual statements we might make about that thing. In this way, the correspondence theorist ensures that there is a reality for every fact and a fact for every reality.

Numerous objections to this approach spring to mind. First, it appears to be a classic case of forcing the facts to fit a theory. The correspondence theorist who takes this metaphysical approach wants the world to contain things that correspond to truths. He cannot find those things in the world, so he simply postulates whatever he thinks he needs. To use a law enforcement analogy, he plants the evidence. But the fact that his theory requires the world to contain certain things provides no evidence that it actually contains them. If the existence of the postulated entities cannot be independently corroborated, the theory would seem to rest on pretty shaky ground.

For the sake of argument, let us suppose that God exists, that heaven is full of Platonic Ideas, and that everything here on Earth possesses the required nature or essence. Would this suffice to rescue the correspondence theory of truth? I do not believe it would. Even with all those postulates in place, the same problems we noted earlier occur, and the same logical chasms open up.

Consider these essences or natures that things are supposed to have. If a thing has a certain nature, then the nature guarantees what the thing will or would do, under all possible circumstances. But if the nature exists, then we can ask the same questions about it that we would normally ask about the thing. Given that the nature has always acted in a certain way, to guarantee a certain kind of result, how do we know that it will continue to act that way? In any given contra-factual scenario, how do we know what the nature would do? Must the nature have its own nature to guarantee what the nature would do? What, then, guarantees the behavior of the nature's nature? No matter how many steps we take along this regress, the original problem remains. The thing, its nature, and its nature's nature, are all equally a part of what is. But between what is and what would be lies that logical chasm. Adding essences to the world's furniture does not make the chasm go away.

Now consider how God would underwrite morality. As soon as God decrees his moral edicts, they become a part of what is. It then becomes intelligible to ask, "Are those edicts good?" Questioning God's law might be immodest. It might also be imprudent, since God could send us to hell. But there is nothing logically improper about the question, "Are God's edicts good?" Denying that the edicts are good would not involve us in a contradiction, for one could coherently suppose that God's edicts ought to have been different. Most people, of course, would suppose nothing of the sort. Whether from modesty, prudence, or piety, they would accept that God's edicts ought to be just as they are. But the decision to embrace God's edicts is not logically forced. It still requires that extra nonlogical step involving faith and a choice of values. Even in a world ruled by God, "is" would not imply "ought." Hume's chasm would still open up whenever we tried to leap from one to the other.

Do not say that God's edicts are good "by definition." No one is under any obligation to accept that definition. And please do not say, "We must accept God's edicts because they are written, as it were, on the tablets of our souls." One could still ask whether the contents of our souls were entirely good. The Humean chasm does not go away.

In Plato's dialogue, *Euthyphro*, Socrates asked Euthyphro whether various actions are pious because they are beloved by the gods, or whether they are beloved by the gods because they are pious. One could ask a similar question about God's moral edicts. Are they good because God made them, or did God make them because they were good? Neither option works out well for the correspondence theorist. If God made the edicts because they were good, then the edicts are not what determine goodness. The foundations of morality lie outside God's laws. But if they are only good because God made them, then the edicts are perfectly arbitrary.

In that case, nothing prevents us from believing that God would have done better to decree some other set of edicts.

A *Euthyphro*-like question also arises with regard to the Platonic Ideas. Is two plus two equal to four because the Ideas are the way they are, or do the Ideas have to be a certain way because two plus two is four? Here one feels inclined to give a definitive answer. Two plus two must be four. It is inconceivable that it should make three, or five, or anything but four. S(3) expresses a logically necessary truth. It would be true no matter how the Platonic Ideas arranged themselves. It would be true even if there were no such Ideas. But if this is correct, then the Ideas would not explain the fact of S(3), even if they existed. They could not underwrite S(3)'s truth. So postulating the Ideas does nothing for us.

It might be time to admit that the correspondence theory is based on a mistake. The correspondence theory holds that truth consists in saying that what is, is, and that what is not, is not. But the plain fact of the matter is that some truths do not even try to say what is or is not. Some try to say what would be, or what could be, or what should be. "Would," "could," and "should" statements are logically distinct from "is" statements. Forcing them all to fit the "is" model does not work, even if we try to shoehorn them all in by making extra metaphysical assumptions. So while the correspondence theory does capture something important about our common-sense notion of truth (truth is what connects with reality in the right way), the theory is still a failure. We have to abandon it.

3

At this point we might be tempted to give up in despair. Maybe the class of truths does not have any underlying unity. That truths come in many irreducible varieties might represent the final word on the subject.

Imagine what would happen if we set out to define the term "bear." We announce that what we seek is the fundamental, underlying unity of the class of bears. We want to know what it is that all bears have in common, the principle that makes them all bears. Now suppose we include in the class of bears all of the following: black bears, brown bears, grizzly bears, polar bears, teddy bears, Chicago Bears, Bad News Bears, and stock market bears. For good measure, we will throw in cartoon bears: Yogi, Boo Boo, Pooh …. Our task would be hopeless. Given all the bears in our sample, there is no unity among them for us to find. To insist on a unity would be foolish.

Perhaps it is equally foolish to seek unity amidst the diversity of truths. To insist that there must be a unity might be just so much Platonizing nonsense.

Wittgenstein provided the key insight. In his *Philosophical Investigations*, he warned readers not to assume that every class has some common essence in which all class members participate. In many instances, the common thread linking the members is not some deep fundamental unity, but a network of "family resemblances." His example was the class of games. There are board games, ball games, card games, dice games, and so on. The sports at the Winter Olympics are all games. Some, like speed skating, are races.

Others, like figure skating, are performances. Most games involve competition, but not all. A child who hits a tennis ball against a backboard, trying to go as many hits as she can without missing, is playing a kind of game, even though she competes against no one but herself. In the card game called solitaire, the player does not even compete against herself. She simply moves her cards around in order to achieve a specified objective. Is there supposed to be some common essence in which all these games participate? We should not assume that there is. We need to look and see, as Wittgenstein urged. Consider what he said about tools:

> Imagine someone's saying "*All* tools serve to modify something. Thus the hammer modifies the position of the nail, the saw the shape of the board, and so on."—And what is modified by the rule, the glue-pot, the nails?—"Our knowledge of a thing's length, the temperature of the glue, the solidity of the box." Would anything be gained by this assimilation of expressions?[7]

The answer to Wittgenstein's question is, of course, "No." Nothing would be gained. We can, if we like, define a tool as that which modifies something. But think of the huge variety of objects that now count as tools. By this definition, a copy of today's newspaper is a tool. It modifies our knowledge of current events. A jump rope is a tool, since it modifies our level of fitness. A chair is also a tool. It modifies the position of one's posterior. Even the meat in my freezer is a tool. It modifies my hunger. If we ponder all this variety, we begin to feel as though our definition has failed us. It does not reveal any real unity among tools. It just papers over the differences among them by forcing all to fit the preferred formula.

I have argued that the correspondence theory of truth does the same thing. It tries to force all truths to fit an inappropriate model. But is there any such thing as an appropriate model? Some classes do not lend themselves to definition, at least not the kind of definition Socrates would enjoy; the kind that reveals the fundamental unity of a class. The class of games resists definition in this way, as does the class of tools. The class of bears is even more disparate. So we need to take Wittgenstein's warning to heart. He is, after all, one of our masters. It will not kill us to drink a little of his tea. We should at least consider the possibility that truths cannot all fit into any one mold. In fact, judging by what we have seen so far, truths appear to be as disparate as bears. Historical truths, scientific truths, mathematical truths, and moral truths do not seem any more similar to one another than do grizzly bears, Chicago Bears, and teddy bears. Perhaps that is all there is to say on the matter.

Maybe we should not give up so easily. Wittgenstein did not claim that all classes are like the class of games. All he said was that, in any given case, we need to look and see for ourselves. Some classes do exhibit a fundamental unity. Think of the class of gold atoms. All gold atoms have something very important in common: each and every one has seventy-nine protons in its nucleus. This feature unites the class and determines all of gold's observable properties. It is thus possible to give a very Socratic definition of gold: "Gold is the metal whose atoms all contain exactly seventy-nine protons in their nuclei." That this should be the defining property of gold is not exactly obvious to common sense. Human beings handled gold and were fascinated by it for thousands of years before anyone discovered the periodic table. The discovery that gold consists of atoms that in turn consist of protons, electrons, and neutrons took a great deal of work. So maybe, just maybe, and despite the appearances, truths resemble gold more than they do games or bears. Maybe the class of truths does have some unity to it, heretofore undiscovered, and maybe we can find it. Why not look and see for ourselves?

4

What should a Socratic definition of truth look like? Obviously it has to identify what all truths have in common, the fundamental principle that makes them all truths. This principle, whatever it is, has to segregate truths both from falsehoods and from nonsense. The principle has to remain faithful to our common-sense notion of truth. It must unpack that notion. The principle should also abstain from making metaphysical presumptions. The definition of truth should not create a bias towards particular truths. It should not come with a built-in preference for any special "ism," be it Platonism, theism, materialism, or what have you. Yet, we cannot content ourselves with a vacuous formula like "truths are what state facts." We want the definition to have some meat on its bones. It should tell us something we did not already know. What gets unpacked from common sense may be—indeed, it will have to be—something that we did not realize was in there.

There is the rub. The principle that unites all truths must be something unfamiliar. Were we familiar with it already, there would be no need for the present inquiry. The principle would simply jump into our heads and we would be done. But since the principle is an unknown, it presents us with a puzzle. We just do not know what this alleged principle could possibly be. It cannot, for example, be that all truths have the same subject matter. Truths are about many different things. Some concern history, others express natural laws, and so on. It is not even accurate to say that all truths are about reality. In what sense could S(3)′ be "about" reality? Reality has to fit into the picture somehow, but it will not do so by becoming the ultimate subject of all true sentences. The principle cannot be about the form of truths either. We have already discovered that truths display an irreducible variety of logical forms. The principle we seek has to leave that variety intact.

If the principle has nothing to do with either form or matter, then it must have something to do with function. Remember Aristotle's four causes: there were material causes, formal causes, efficient causes, and final causes. One might suppose that the material cause of a truth would be its physical substratum—the paper and ink it appears on, the breath with which it is spoken, or perhaps the zeros and ones of the computer into which it is typed. For our purposes, however, it is better to think not of the physics, but more abstractly, of the semantics. From this perspective, the material cause of a truth is its subject matter, including in that all the things, real or imaginary, to which the truth refers. At the same abstract level, the formal cause of a truth is not the grammatical form of the sentence expressing it, but rather its logical form. The efficient cause of a truth, at any level, is simply the speaker, the person who puts the truth into words. The final cause of a truth is the purpose it serves. The creations of rational beings serve their purpose by performing their designated functions. A hammer serves its purpose by banging in nails, a car by getting us to work on time, and so on. Truths, considered as expressions of our rational nature, are like this. With respect to any particular truth, we express it for a reason. We want that truth to do its job, to play its role in our language game (there is Wittgenstein's influence again).

Truths display a wide and irreducible variety of both material and formal causes. Since the world contains billions of speakers, truths have many efficient causes as well. If there is any unifying principle for truth, our only hope of finding it is to look at final causes. Perhaps there is some one goal all truths reach, a single function all truths perform.

Things do not look good. One can feel the hope slipping away. We cannot assume the existence of a common goal, accomplished through some unifying function. We have to look and see. But when we look, all we seem to find is more diversity. There are billions of speakers, each with his or her unique set of goals. The range of purposes served by human language is as wide as the range of human needs and human desires.

We enunciate truths to air our opinions and express our feelings. We enunciate them to persuade others to believe things, to think things, and to do things. We use truths to seduce, motivate, and frighten. Truths have many uses. Yet we cannot equate the true with the useful, as the pragmatists do, because lies are useful too. Lies are often more useful than truths. That is why people lie.

Things do not get any better when we look at functions. A little introspection should show that there is no one action our minds perform whenever we say something true. It is not as if some bell in our heads rang every time our cognitive faculties got something right. Our cognitive faculties can "get it right" in a lot of different ways and by doing a lot of different things. Once again we have sought unity, only to find ourselves afloat in a sea of plurality.

So, is it time to give up our Socratic quest and become disquotationalists? Disquotationalism analyzes the meaning of the word "true" by pointing out that the sentence "P is true" is equivalent to asserting the proposition "P." "P is true" is true if and only if "P" is true. And this is simply because P is true if and only if P. According to disquotationalism, there is not much more to say about truth than that. As far as it goes, disquotationalism seems fine. But it really doesn't go anywhere, does it? It does not even try to answer the important question, which is this: "For any P, if P is true, what makes it true?" Given the disquotationalist account of truth, we can and should still ask how propositions acquire their truth values.

So, once again, we should resolve not to give up so easily. There has to be a way to answer the question just put, and it may still be possible to answer it by constructing a Socratic definition of truth. We have not proven such a definition to be impossible. We have only shown that it cannot rely on certain things. It cannot rely on the material, formal, or efficient causes of truth. The definition could identify a final cause of truth, but if it does, the cause in question cannot be an element of mental contents.

If the function we seek cannot be mental, then it has to be something purely logical. If there is a unifying principle to truth, it must be some purely logical function that all truths perform and that no falsehood performs.

"If there is a unifying principle to truth …" I understand how big that "if" is. We have not proven that the principle exists. We have only clung to the hope of finding it, while winnowing down the number of places it might be. Perhaps, with just a little more looking ….

5

I think we can find a good Socratic definition of truth. In the coming sections I will develop and defend such a definition. But since we have tried to heed Wittgenstein's warnings on this subject, perhaps we should also heed the warning of another master, Soren Kierkegaard:

> If Hegel had written the whole of his *Logic* and then said … that it was merely an experiment

in thought … then he would certainly have been the greatest thinker who had ever lived. As it is, he is merely comic.[8]

I cannot hope to be either the greatest thinker ever, or the most foolish. There is too much competition at both ends of the spectrum. However, let us agree to call my definition of truth a thought experiment. What if the experiment fails? With any luck there will be no shortage of critics to tell me where I went wrong. Being neither a PhD nor a trial lawyer, I will be free to admit my error and move on. This is where being a philosopher works to my advantage. As noted earlier, philosophy is a tolerant mistress. She does not make us pay for our mistakes. When we err, the tigers do not eat us.

In this case, the potential cost of error is even less than usual. No one needs a Socratic definition of truth. We can all tell truth from falsity well enough without one, just as we can do competent arithmetic without grasping the essence of Number. Even a poor definition of truth would do no harm. Mistakes regarding the concept of truth would not necessarily cascade into other branches of philosophy. Ethics, metaphysics, and epistemology could go on just as before, without the slightest hint of infection.

Normally, when we assert or deny propositions, we do not even employ our concept of truth. To affirm that Socrates was a man, we require concepts for "Socrates" and "man," since those are the concepts explicitly deployed in that proposition. Other concepts may be involved implicitly. For example, if our concept of

Socrates contains a reference to Greece, then the concept "Greece" becomes a prerequisite for understanding the proposition "Socrates was a man." But the concept of truth is not in any similar way a prerequisite. If we understand, and can competently employ, such concepts as "man," "woman," "Socrates," and "Greece," then we already possess all the tools needed to either assert or deny that Socrates was a man. Invoking the concept of truth, even covertly, would be superfluous. The concept of truth is not essential to affirmation and denial; it is instead something we construct on top of our already existing practice of offering and rejecting indicative sentences. We arrive at that concept by reflecting on what constitutes proper employment for all other concepts. Truth is in that sense a second order concept. This explains why a confused notion of truth doesn't (usually) corrupt our judgments, either in philosophy, or in any other discipline.

Still, it would be a fine thing if my experiment succeeded. It would represent progress up the ladder. To say that our concept of truth is frequently dormant is not to say that we never have any use for it. We can, actually, make excellent use of it. Concepts are the spectacles through which philosophers view the world. To develop a sharper conception of truth would thus be like having night vision goggles for the cave.

6

The solution to our puzzle, or at least a clue to the solution, lies in a remark made in section 2. Reality, I said, is not big enough to underwrite the claim made in the sample sentence S(2). If we think about that remark, the solution just falls right out. All we need is something that is big enough. But what could be greater than reality? Reality includes, well, everything, does it not? Yes, of course it does. It includes literally everything in heaven and Earth, everything that exists now, or ever has existed, or ever will exist. The actions that real entities perform, the events they become involved in, the properties they possess, the relations they bear to one another, it's all in there. This totality of all things we call the real world. Let $\mathbf{W}_r$ be our theoretical symbol for it.

$\mathbf{W}_r$ is the real world. It is the only real world. By definition, it is a unique entity. Of course, we often use the term "world" to refer to something smaller. For example, we might refer to "this world," meaning the material universe, and put that in contrast to "the next world," meaning heaven and hell. Or we might speak of "this world," meaning our existence on this particular planet named Earth, which would then be contrasted with "other worlds," meaning civilizations on distant planets. By $\mathbf{W}_r$, however, I mean something all-inclusive: heaven, hell, Earth, other planets, the whole material universe, plus any other universes there are, whether we can ever know about them or not. Conceived of in this way, no real entity, no actually existing thing, can stand outside $\mathbf{W}_r$, not even God. So what could be bigger than $\mathbf{W}_r$?[9]

$\mathbf{W}_r$ may be the only actual world, but it is not the only possible world. Possible worlds are legion. Our imaginations can conjure up a potentially infinite variety of them. We can imagine worlds where space has more than three dimensions, or fewer. We can imagine worlds containing dragons, elves, and hobbits. We can imagine worlds in which Harold defeats William at Hastings, in which the Confederacy wins the Civil War, in which the Roman Empire never falls. The laws of nature do not have to be as modern science conceives them. If "possible" means "logically possible," so that a possible world is any world that may be coherently conceived, then clearly we may coherently conceive of laws quite different from those that actually pertain. We can imagine gravity to work according to an inverse cube rule, instead of the actual inverse square. For all the difference it makes to logic, the world does not have to operate according to gravity at all. The physical world might be ruled by some other principle. The physical constants discovered by science could have different values. Some could be variables rather than constants. The periodic table does not have to be a block of rows and columns. It could just as easily be a pyramid or a circle. Plants and animals could sprout forth via acts of supernatural creation, instead of evolving through natural selection. The imagination is a powerful thing. Its possibilities are endless.

Some fictional worlds are important enough to philosophy to warrant their own symbols. $W_{\varnothing}$, for example, is the world where there is nothing. I do mean nothing. $W_{\varnothing}$, the null world, contains neither minds nor bodies. It does not even contain empty space. There is nothing there. There is not even a "there" there. Philosophers sometimes ask why there is something rather than nothing. This is equivalent to asking why $W_\emptyset$ and W_r are not one and the same.

If we can ask why anything exists, then we might equally well ask, "Why doesn't everything exist?" Why, in other words, is not every logical possibility realized? Imagine a world that contains within itself a replica of every other possible world. Each sub-world inside this mega-world would be segregated from all the others. There would be no connection between them, no interaction among them. Each would exist in total isolation. This mega-world would be like an enormous mansion, with an infinite number of rooms, with no doors or windows to any of the rooms (and no air vents either). Let the symbol for this hypothetical place be W_Ω.

Worlds like W_Ω, which have two or more unassociated parts, are called "multi-worlds." The parts of a multi-world, the rooms inside the mansion, would be sub-worlds. The real world could be a multi-world, for all we know. Our sub-world might be just one of many. But there is no way for us to find out. The definition of the multi-world bars us from ever discovering that we live in one. So if W_r could be a multi-world, then it could also be a super multi-world like W_Ω. Since we can never know if that is the case, we have to remain agnostic.[10]

The symbol W with a subscript names a particular world. W with no subscript symbolizes the class of all possible worlds. Its membership includes W_r, $W_\emptyset$, W_Ω, and all the rest. I apologize for all these symbols. There are only a few more after this. Think of W's members as being greater or lesser modifications of W_r. Consider how the video image of a face can be altered by insensible gradations. Looking at first like a Caucasian woman's face, it transforms into an Asian woman's face, and then into a man's. Afterwards it looks like a monkey's face, a cat's, or a sparrow's. Our world bears the same relation to fictional worlds as the original video face bore to the alternatives. Each successive modification of W_r's "face" would be a fictional world. But whereas the video face is two dimensional and changes through ordinary time, W_r's face is a four-dimensional thing that changes only in our conception. It changes, if you will, through imaginary time. And while the features of the video face can always be visualized, W_r's "face" includes many abstract features and intangible properties that have no pictorial representation.

The view that fantasy worlds represent successive modifications of our world suggests a method for putting worlds in order. We can conceive of the members of W as being arranged in a logical space. Worlds close together in this space resemble each other closely and possess similar sets of properties. Worlds farther apart are less similar. Lines through W's logical space follow paths of possible modification. We can even think of W_r as occupying the origin where all the axes of logical space meet. Any curve emerging from the origin represents a way of modifying reality in imaginary time.

The logical space occupied by W's membership may have as many dimensions as you please. There are, after all, an indefinitely large number of directions in which reality might be modified. However, in the interest of simplicity, we might want to limit the space to just two dimensions. Visualize a circle in a plane. Each point inside the circle represents a possible world, a member of **W**. The points beyond the circle collectively constitute the realm of incoherence—the land of logical chaos. It is where two plus two equals five, where objects are black and white and also red all over. Outside the circle, the points do not represent discrete individual worlds. Where logic does not apply, worlds cannot individuate themselves, so the whole realm is just one big, jumbled, confusing mess.

The circle itself does not belong either to the order within, or to the chaos without. It is the boundary between the two. Making the circle a kind of no man's land has this advantage: it allows us to avoid placing any particular set of possible worlds at the boundary. Since all possible worlds are equally coherent, none is any more at the edge of logical chaos than any another. Putting some at the edge, rather than others, would be arbitrary.

To be fair, we might make our diagram an ellipse rather than a circle. W_r would stand at one focus of the ellipse, W_o at the other. If the field of possible worlds can represent all the different ways of modifying reality, then it can with equal justice be thought of as representing all the different ways of adding clutter to nothingness. An ellipse thus creates the right balance.

Here is one more symbol: **B**. This symbol stands for the whole plane in which our ellipse rests. I call this the "plane of being." It includes real being (W_r), non-being (all other worlds), and un-being (the realm of incoherence).

The correspondence theory failed because it focused exclusively on reality, and reality was not big enough to bear the burden that the theory placed on it. But we now have at our disposal a conceptual tool vastly greater than reality. Reality, $\mathbf{W}_r$, is a mere speck inside the cavernous domain of $\mathbf{B}$. $\mathbf{B}$ encompasses literally everything—what is, what could be, and even what cannot be. It is truly that than which nothing greater can be conceived. With this monster of a concept in our conceptual toolbox, constructing a workable theory of truth becomes feasible. We can also have some fun with it.

7

Think again of that sequence of video images. The original face in the picture was that of a Caucasian woman. One way to alter the picture is to change the structure of the face: the cheekbones can be raised or lowered, the nose broadened or made narrower, and so on. Another method of alteration is to change the orientation of the face. The face can be rotated either clockwise or counter-clockwise until it appears upside down. We could also rotate the face along a different axis, until the woman appears to be facing away from the camera. Each rotation of the face creates a new perspective and a new picture. We can thus have an entire series of faces that are structurally identical to each other, yet each belongs to a different picture, because each represents a different way of modifying the original picture.

The same principle applies to worlds. We could have a set of worlds such that each member of the set was structurally identical to every other member. Yet each set member would be a distinct world, because it would represent a different way of modifying this one. For example, we could have a set of mega-worlds, all just like W_Ω, each representing a different modification of W_r. The sequence of mega-worlds, $W_{\Omega 1}, W_{\Omega 2}, W_{\Omega 3}, \ldots$, would appear as an arc drawn across W's ellipse.

With worlds, as with pictures, perspective matters. The difference between speaking the truth and uttering a falsehood often depends on the speaker's perspective. It depends, in other words, on the frame of reference from which the speaker observes the world. This aspect of world theory will be important to the theory of propositions, which is coming up shortly.

There is no such thing as the set of worlds structurally similar to $W_\emptyset$. There may be an infinite number of ways to have everything, but there is only one way to have nothing. Nothingness cannot be rotated. We cannot look at it in different ways, or from different angles. There is nothing there to look at, or to rotate.

8

Think again of S(1). For any speaker inside our frame of reference, which includes everybody currently living on the planet Earth, S(1) would be true. S(1), then, is true of W_r. Now let the world change slowly through imaginary time. There are many small alterations that would not affect S(1)'s truth value. S(1) would remain an accurate description of affairs as long as the world's "face" did not stray too far from reality. At some point, however, the accumulation of changes would become too great. Perhaps William would disappear from the scene, or Harold would die before becoming King of England, or maybe the two men would appear as allies rather than enemies. S(1)'s truth value would then be compromised.

Picture in your mind the line segment we just traversed through **W**. At one end of the segment lies our starting point, W_r. At the other end is the point of falsification, the point at which S(1) ceases to be true. W_r belongs to the segment; the point of falsification does not. Do you remember how we drew segments like this in middle-school math class? We would draw a line. At one end we would put a solid dot, at the other, a small, open circle. The solid dot would belong to the segment. Every point after the dot would also belong to the segment, up to, but not including, the point represented by the open circle. In this case, W_r is the solid dot, while the open circle signifies the point of falsification.

Let us repeat this thought experiment until every possible line segment emanating from W_r has been drawn. We would end up with something that looks like a Venn diagram. The sheet of paper would represent **B**, the formidable plane of being. The sheet would be blank except for two items. First, there would be the ellipse constituting **W**. Second, inside the ellipse, there would be a dark mass of points representing all the worlds for which S(1) would be true. S(1) would accurately describe things, if any of those darkened points were W_r.

The points inside the dark mass all have something important in common. They constitute a natural class.

Let us designate that class M[S(1)]. All other points inside the ellipse will be members of another class, namely N[S(1)]. Points lying outside the ellipse do not represent possible worlds, and so cannot belong to either M or N.

One of the logical functions of S(1) is thus to divide the worlds of **B** into two classes: an M class and an N class. We will call this the "cut" that S(1) makes in **B**. The speaker of S(1) does not consciously, or even unconsciously, perform the cutting. The cut is not a psychological phenomenon. It is a purely logical function of the statement.

Other people might speak or write sentences that make the same cut. Those sentences might be verbatim duplicates of S(1), or they might be close English paraphrases of it. They could be sentences in other languages, such as French, German, or Chinese. If two statements make the same cut, then they are equivalent, and they may be said to express the same proposition.

A moment ago we allowed ourselves to employ the word "true" when identifying the M of a statement. That was sloppy. The word "true" should not get embedded in the definition of truth. We can clean that up and add a bit more rigor to the presentation with the following series of definitions:

> A "statement" is a sentence or group of sentences issued by a given speaker from some given frame of reference. A statement may be of any length. There is no preset maximum or minimum number of words a statement may contain.

Let there be a statement S. M[S] is a class of possible worlds linked to S. To say of any given world W that it belongs to M[S] is to say that if W = $\mathbf{W}_r$, then S. The membership of M[S] includes all worlds that satisfy that condition, and only those worlds. If a given world does not belong to M[S], then it belongs to N[S].

The "cut" of a statement S is the way S divides the worlds of **B** into an M and an N. Two statements make the same cut in **B** if they have the same M and N.

Two statements are "equivalent" if they make the same cut.

A "proposition" is the class of all statements equivalent to a given statement.

To these definitions we can add an axiom:

A proposition has the same M and N that its members do. It makes the same cut in **B** that they do.

To say of a proposition that it has a certain M is simply to say that its members all have that M. Likewise, to say that a proposition cuts **B** in a certain way is to say no more than that its members make that cut. The axiom creates a linguistic convenience that permits us to talk very abstractly regarding the logically relevant properties of entire statement classes.

We can now offer the following Socratic definition of truth:

> Truth is the class of all propositions that contain $\mathbf{W}_r$ in their Ms.

This is the containment theory of truth. It accomplishes everything we set out to achieve. It concisely identifies the underlying unity of truth, and it does so without taking any particular truths for granted. The definition makes no metaphysical presumptions. Its conception of "reality," or $\mathbf{W}_r$, is open-ended enough to allow for many different metaphysical interpretations. The definition links truth to reality, in accordance with our common-sense notion of truth, but it does not insist that truth have any essential connection to the mind. Containment theory does not require propositions to have real members. It does not even require that propositions be expressible in any human language, or in any finite number of words. There are some propositions only God would understand, yet containment theory does not assume that God exists. It does not assume that anyone exists. If $\mathbf{W}_r$ were uninhabited, many propositions would still be true, even though the members of those propositions would all be fictions. According to containment theory, not only is truth independent of our desires, it is independent of our very existence. The theory is thus free of any anthropocentric taint.[11]

Constructing this definition was relatively easy. The hard part will be defending it. We still need to show how the unity just presented connects with the plurality we examined in previous sections. We must also demonstrate that true propositions do not contain $\mathbf{W}_r$ in their Ms just by accident. On the contrary—true propositions are true *because* they contain $\mathbf{W}_r$ in their Ms. The whole point of containment theory is to explain what makes a true proposition true. Identifying the class of truths is actually a byproduct of that explanatory effort. But the explanatory value of containment theory is itself something that will have to be explained.

9

$\mathbf{W}_r$ is the title our world bears. It is not our world's name. The distinction is easy to grasp. "Barack Obama" is our president's name. "President of the United States" is his title. Referring to our world as "$\mathbf{W}_r$" is thus analogous to calling Barack Obama "Mr. President."

We can provide every possible world with a title, even though there are an infinite number of them. When a world has no other name, let its title be $\mathbf{W}_{x,y}$, where x and y are the world's coordinates in the plane of being. For convenience, let $\mathbf{W}_\varnothing$ lie at the origin. $\mathbf{W}_r$ will lie someplace to the right of $\mathbf{W}_\varnothing$, along the X axis. All other worlds are deployed on the plane according to some metric of similarity, forming an ellipse. A world's properties determine its location on the plane, provided that we include amongst its properties relational features such as "rotation" relative to this world.

Now consider the proposition "$\mathbf{W}_{0,0}$ is $\mathbf{W}_r$." We will call this the null proposition, or $P^\varnothing$. $\mathbf{W}_{0,0}$ is just another name for $W_\varnothing$, so $P^\varnothing$ basically asserts that the null world is the real world, that there is nothing rather than something. Think about how $P^\varnothing$ stands in relation to our first sample sentence, S(1). Does it entail S(1)? No. Actually it entails not-S(1), for if nothing exists, then neither do Harold or William, so S(1) cannot be true. But if $P^\varnothing$ entails not-S(1), then according to the definitions given earlier, $W_\varnothing$ belongs to both N[S(1)] and M[not-S(1)].

We have not given our world, W_r, a name. Let us just call it "$W_{n,0}$" to indicate that it is somewhere on the x axis of our plane of being. The value of n will be left undetermined (determining a value would require both a precise metric for assigning coordinates and a complete list of W_r's properties, neither of which we have). Our hypothetical name for W_r permits us to construct the proposition "$W_{n,0}$ is W_r". This proposition, P^n, entails S(1). If our world is the real world, then S(1) is true. In our world, William does defeat Harold at Hastings. $W_{n,0}$ thus belongs to M[S(1)].

The reader can now see how the M of a statement gets constructed. Just think of all the propositions having the form "$W_{x,y}$ is W_r." Given any statement S, some of these propositions will entail S, and some will not. When one of these propositions does entail S, the world named by that proposition will belong to M[S]. S is then true if and only if M[S] contains the world that happens to be W_r. That is containment theory in a nutshell.

Here is another complementary way of looking at things. The class of true propositions is the class of all propositions entailed by P^n. P^n entails every true proposition, including itself. It entails no falsehoods. We cannot define truth this way, because P^n is not true by definition. It merely happens to be true. However, given that the world is what it is, the class of truths does in fact coincide with the logical posterity of P^n. If God, in his infinite simplicity, were to spend eternity contemplating just one proposition, P^n would be it.

Our analysis oversimplifies matters by assuming that statements are never vague. Of course, the statements we make in daily life often do get vague at the edges, and for those it would sometimes be indeterminate whether or not a given world belonged to the M of a particular S. For heuristic purposes we may ignore vagueness. Just as physicists sometimes ignore friction, and economists talk as if people were totally rational, so we may speak as if all statements were perfectly clear. Their frequent lack of clarity in no way undermines our theory. The theory works, even if cuts through **B** are often made with dull knives.

It is also no objection that the concept of **B** is itself vague. We have not specified any metric of similarity that would precisely locate every world at a specific point on the plane. We could not do that even if we wanted to, nor could we really construct the Ms of propositions using the infinitely laborious method described. But none of that matters. We are not trying to describe how real flesh-and-blood people might go about distinguishing truths from falsehoods. We are instead trying to say what truth fundamentally is. All the operations involved here are purely logical. If we can describe them, there is no need to carry them out.

Consider this analogy. Suppose we were to define gold as the element whose atoms contained seventy-nine protons in their nuclei. Now imagine someone objecting to our definition by pointing out how useless and impractical it is. "We cannot possibly count all those protons," he exclaims. "That would take forever!" He is right, of course, but his point is moot. He has mistaken our intentions. We never meant to provide a practical method for identifying gold, something to be used by miners, jewelers, and coin dealers. We only wanted to position gold within the conceptual framework of modern chemistry. Our project regarding truth is similar. We are not trying to tell real people how to avoid being deceived. Rather, we are trying to place truth within a philosophical framework by uncovering truth's Socratic unity. And that is what (I claim) containment theory has done.

10

We have already seen how two statements that differ in their physical composition can express the same proposition. A written version of S(1) may express the same proposition as a spoken version, though one consists of marks on paper, the other of vibrations in the air. Other written versions could also express that same proposition, even though they might be written using different words, in different languages, on different types of paper, or with different colored ink.

A corollary to this idea is that physically identical statements might express entirely different propositions.

Imagine that somewhere in another galaxy there is a planet remarkably like Earth. The planet has an oxygen-rich atmosphere. Plants, animals, and even human beings live there. The history of this planet follows a course eerily similar to that of Earth, right up until the year 1066. The histories of the two planets then diverge. On Earth, William defeats Harold at Hastings and becomes King of England. On the other planet, "Earth Two," Harold wins the battle. Now imagine someone on Earth Two speaking words exactly like those found in S(1). This person is as human as we are. He speaks English. He understands what he is saying. Yet his statement would be false. How can his statement be false, when physically identical statements made on Earth are true? The person on Earth Two speaks from a different frame of reference than we do. Because of this, his words mean something different. They refer to a different William, a different Harold, and a different battle. Those words express a proposition unrelated to the proposition we express using similar words.

So a form of words can be true when spoken by one person, false when spoken by another. Does this mean that truth is relative? No. The truth value of a proposition is invariant. A proposition cannot be true relative to one person, but false relative to another. It cannot be true at one moment in time and then become false at a later date. If a proposition is true, then it is always true, for everyone. Something does depend on a speaker's frame of reference. The words "William defeated Harold" will be true if spoken by an Earthling, false if spoken by some denizen of Earth Two. But we shouldn't focus on the words; what matter are the propositions being expressed. The proposition we express when we claim that William conquered England is true. It was true a million years ago, and it will still be true a million years hence. It is true not only for us, but for everyone who lives on Earth Two. That the people on Earth Two are unfamiliar with this proposition makes no difference. The same goes for the proposition they express when they assert that William lost at Hastings. The truth value of their proposition is also invariant. It is true for us, even though we know nothing of it.

Consider the analogy with modern physics. According to Einstein's theory of relativity, many things are relative. The mass, length, and velocity of an object all depend to some extent on who is observing it. The statement that a given object is moving is, by itself, virtually meaningless. One has to ask, "Moving relative to whom?" Yet even relativity theory recognizes some constants. The speed of light, for example, is the same for all. More generally, the laws of nature apply equally to everyone, regardless of their frame of reference.

The truth values of propositions are among the constants in a relativistic world. Imagine that the reader and I are traveling through space in different ships. Off in the distance we see a third ship. Is the third ship moving? It all depends. Perhaps it is stationary relative to me, but moving relative to the reader. If I say, "That ship over there is moving," I have spoken a falsehood. If the reader says those exact same words, she will be speaking the truth. So here again the truth value of some form of words is relative, and context is everything. Yet there is nothing relative about the truth values of our propositions. The proposition that the reader has expressed about that third ship is true, even for me. I could express the same proposition by asserting that the third ship was moving through the reader's frame of reference. If the proposition was true when the reader expressed it, then it will also be true when I express it. Whether the third ship is moving depends upon the observer. But whether a given ship is moving relative to a given observer is not itself relative to any observer.

It is a part of our common sense notion of truth that truth is universal. We want to believe that what is true for us is true for everybody and that what was true once will be true forever. Containment theory preserves this aspect of common sense. It does so by distinguishing clearly between propositions and forms of words. Given this distinction, we can maintain our common-sense view of truth, even in a world like ours, where many things are relative.

11

A proposition is true if and only if it contains $\mathbf{W}_r$ in its M. So let P^1 be the proposition that twenty-first-century English-speaking Earthlings would express with a statement such as $S(1)$. P^1 is true, and it contains $\mathbf{W}_r$ in its M. $\mathbf{W}_r$ falls inside the shaded sector of $\mathbf{B}$ created by P^1's cut. Furthermore, P^1 is true *because* it contains $\mathbf{W}_r$ in its M. It is true, in short, because its description of affairs is appropriate not just for some set of fictional worlds, but also for this world, the real world. The features of reality explain why P^1 is true.

Had reality been different, P^1 would have been false. So the truth of P^1 and the placement of $\mathbf{W}_r$ within its M do not just happen to coincide. The two are essentially connected, and it was this essential connection that we were looking to capture in our definition.

The relation of $\mathbf{W}_r$ to P^1 seems fairly clear. The same relation will hold between $\mathbf{W}_r$ and any other historical claim. The location of $\mathbf{W}_r$ within the claim's M or N will be essentially connected to that claim's truth or falsity. Will this model hold up when we examine other types of claims? That remains to be seen. However, before we can tackle that project, we have a few loose ends to tie up with regard to propositions and possible worlds.

How does $\mathbf{W}_\varnothing$ relate to P^1? It cannot belong to $M[P^1]$. P^1 does not describe any event in that world. The syllogism "If $\mathbf{W}_\varnothing = \mathbf{W}_r$, then P^1" is incorrect. $\mathbf{W}_\varnothing$ therefore belongs to $N[P^1]$. There are, of course, no instances of P^1 in $\mathbf{W}_\varnothing$. $\mathbf{W}_\varnothing$ contains no speakers who could express P^1. This makes no difference. The question is not, "Would P^1 be true if it were expressed in $\mathbf{W}_\varnothing$?" but rather, "Does P^1 offer a fair description of $\mathbf{W}_\varnothing$?" The answer is clearly, "No, it does not." That is why $\mathbf{W}_\varnothing$ belongs to P^1's N.

Now consider the statement, "Nothing exists—not space, not time, not anything." $\mathbf{W}_\varnothing$ would be the only world in that statement's M. All others would belong to its N. Again, it matters not whether such a statement does, or even could, occur in $\mathbf{W}_\varnothing$. There are many things one might say of $\mathbf{W}_\varnothing$, even if there is nothing one could say in it.

Is P^1 true of $\mathbf{W}_\Omega$? Well, there are infinitely many $\mathbf{W}_\Omega$'s: $\mathbf{W}_{\Omega 1}$, $\mathbf{W}_{\Omega 2}$, $\mathbf{W}_{\Omega 3}$ ... and P^1 would be true of some, false for others. Some would belong to $M[P^1]$, others to N[P^1]. "But all of the $\mathbf{W}_\Omega$s are identical!" you say. Yes, they are. Yet each represents a different way of modifying reality. P^1 is true because it refers to our world, where William does defeat Harold at Hastings. So the question to ask of any given $\mathbf{W}_\Omega$ is, which sub-world in that $\mathbf{W}_\Omega$ counts as the homologue of our world? If, in that modified version of $\mathbf{W}_r$, William still defeats Harold at Hastings, then that $\mathbf{W}_\Omega$ belongs to M[P^1]. Otherwise it belongs to N[P^1].

A $\mathbf{W}_\Omega$, by definition, is a world where all possibilities are realized. Somewhere within a $\mathbf{W}_\Omega$ there are herds of unicorns, tribes of elves, and woods full of Sasquatches. Somewhere within each $\mathbf{W}_\Omega$ is a realm of two-dimensional beings like those portrayed in Edwin Abbott's *Flatland*. However, this does not mean that every $\mathbf{W}_\Omega$ belongs to the M of every proposition. If $\mathbf{W}_r$ were one of the $\mathbf{W}_\Omega$'s, that would not render every proposition true. To suppose otherwise would be incoherent. We cannot have a world where P and not-P are both true.

Consider the proposition expressed by the statement "Harold defeated William at Hastings in 1066." Assume this statement to be made by an English-speaking person currently living on Earth. The proposition just identified is false. It would still be false even if $\mathbf{W}_r$ turned out to be one of the $\mathbf{W}_\Omega$'s. Now if $\mathbf{W}_r$ were a $\mathbf{W}_\Omega$, then certainly there would be some sub-world in it where a guy named Harold beats another guy named William at a battle known as Hastings. This fact would, however, be irrelevant. The proposition identified is a proposition about our Harold, the Harold who lived on Earth during the eleventh century. So what happens to other Harolds in other sub-worlds makes no difference. They would be as irrelevant to the proposition as are the Harolds on other planets.

So while a $\mathbf{W}_\Omega$ may be a place where every possibility is realized, it is not a place where every proposition would be true. Many propositions would be false, even of such a world.

12

Let the words contained in S(1) be spoken by a twenty-first-century English-speaking Earthling. Call this fellow "Sam." Now imagine our world being transformed through imaginary time. At the end of the journey, we arrive in a world where the verb "to defeat" means "to be decapitated by." There is a Sam in that world who utters the words in S(1). That Sam—call him "Modified Sam"—is actually claiming that Harold won the battle of Hastings by chopping off William's head. However, in this modified world, William defeats Harold precisely as he does in ours, in the ordinary sense of "defeat."

Does the modified world belong to the M or N of Sam's statement? The correct answer is that it belongs to the M. Sam's statement is true of that world, even though Modified Sam's physically identical statement is not. There is no mystery here. Sam and his modification are simply expressing different propositions. Sam, speaking from the frame of reference provided by Earth, means one thing by his words. Modified Sam, speaking from the referential frame of Modified Earth, means something entirely different.

Context affects meaning. What a person means by his words has a lot to do with where and when he says them. The meaning of the word "defeat," when Sam uses it, is set by the conventions of English usage in Sam's world. What Modified Sam means by "defeat" is set by the conventions prevalent in his (fictional) world.

That Sam and Modified Sam use identical words to express different propositions should surprise no one. We have already seen this principle at work in our discussion of statements made on Earth and Earth Two.

Sam's statement concerning William is true of Modified Earth, even though it seems not to be true in it. This distinction, between being true of and being true in, should also be familiar. We exploited that very distinction only a short time ago, when we discussed the truth values of statements made concerning W_o.

13

These interpretive principles become critical when we consider statements that assert truth or falsity of other statements. Let there be some statement S(5) that asserts the truth of S(1). S(5) and S(1) belong to the same proposition. S(5) will thus be true of any world in which William defeats Harold at Hastings under the conditions S(1) specifies. But what of worlds where the statement called S(1) claims (falsely, let us assume) that the North lost the American Civil War? Won't S(5) be false for those worlds, regardless of what William and Harold do? No, of course not. S(5)'s meaning is fixed by the conditions in this world, the world in which S(5) is made. So it matters not what S(5) would mean if it were uttered in some other world. It only matters what it means in this one, and in this one, S(1) refers to the Battle of Hastings, not to the American Civil War.

Now consider a series of sentences. The first says that the second is true, the second claims that the third is true, the third asserts that the fourth is true, and so on, ad infinitum. The first sentence depends on the second for its meaning. The first asserts whatever proposition the second asserts. The second depends in turn on the third, the third on the fourth, and so on. Since there is no end to the series, the proposition expressed by all these sentences never gets fixed. So no proposition gets expressed. The sentences in the series belong to no proposition at all. There is no truth value to any of them, not even a negative one.

"Wait," the reader might object. "You admit that the second sentence in the series is neither true nor false. Hence it is not true. But the first sentence says that it is true. The first sentence is thus false. By the same reasoning, the second sentence must also be false, since it asserts the truth of the third sentence, which we are agreed is not true. Continuing down the line, we find that all the sentences in the series are false, contrary to what you claimed."

The reader makes a strong case, but I believe he is still mistaken. For any sentence in the series to be false, it has to make a cut in **B**. There are no truth values without cuts. Yet no sentence in the series actually makes a cut. Each one passes the buck, handing off the job of cutting to the next sentence in the series.

So despite appearances, the sentences are not actually false—although none of them is true either, for the same reason.

Next, consider this paradox. Imagine a three-by-five card. On one side of the card there is the sentence "the sentence on the other side of this card is true." On the other side we find this sentence: "The sentence on the other side of this card is false." So if the first sentence is true, then it is false, and if it false, then it is true. Or so it would appear. But, of course, if we perform the same kind of analysis here as we did in the cases above, we find that neither sentence expresses a proposition. Each sentence counts on the other to fix its meaning, so no meaning gets fixed, no cut gets made, and there are no truth values, positive or negative, to be found.

The reader might still feel uncomfortable with this. "What if I said 'The bear in the next room has brown fur,' when in fact there is no bear in the next room. My statement is false, is it not? So if I say, 'The sentence written on the wall in the next room is true,' when there is no sentence on the wall, then that statement should also be false, for exactly the same reason. Yet by your account, the latter statement expresses no proposition, and so is neither true nor false." That is precisely right. The first statement about the bear expresses a proposition. The second one about the sentence on the wall does not. This may seem counter-intuitive, but it represents the simplest possible account of truth asserting statements, and it gives us the easiest way to handle paradoxes, such as the one written on the index card.

Finally, consider sentences that refer to their own truth values. We can apply to these the same principles just used. For example, the sentences "this sentence is false" and "this sentence is true" are neither true nor false. They make no cuts, so they express no propositions. Most self-referential sentences thus provide no special difficulty.

There is, however, a special case worth discussing. How, one might ask, are we to interpret a sentence that says of itself that it is neither true nor false? Consider this especially diabolical version of the problem:

A: Sentence A is either false, or neither true nor false.

Sentence A appears to leave us with no options. It cannot be true, because if it is true, then it is either false, or neither true nor false. It cannot be false either, because if it is false, then it is true. But if it is neither true nor false, then apparently it is true. No matter how we interpret A, we find ourselves stuck with an unresolved and seemingly irresolvable quandary.

The solution is actually quite simple. Sentence A is neither true nor false. It makes no cut. It expresses no proposition. So it is not essentially different from any other self-referring statement. But how can this be, given that it seems so different?

Remember what was said earlier about frames of reference. We showed back in section 10 how a claim can be true when issued from one frame of reference, even though a verbally similar claim, issued from another frame of reference, might be false. We can use that insight here. When we, speaking from our own frames of reference, say of Sentence A that it is neither true nor false, we speak the truth. But when the speaker of A tries to assert the same thing, he ends up expressing no proposition at all. His frame of reference makes nonsense of his words. Uttering A puts him in the wrong position to offer commentary on A's truth value. Of course, the speaker remains "in the wrong position" only as long as he is uttering A. Once he moves on to other sentences, he is back in our frame of reference, and he may make sensible references to A's truth value, just as we can.

What defines a frame of reference is not just the speaker's physical location and velocity, but also his conceptual apparatus, together with his logical location relative to the objects of his discourse. Commenting upon the truth value of the sentence one is currently uttering creates a logical frame of reference which automatically deprives the sentence of propositional content. Context affects meaning, but in the context of self-referential sentences, meaning evaporates.

14

Pretend that you are a proposition. You want very much to be true. Being false would seem humiliating. All the other propositions would laugh at you. Your parents would be so disappointed. You can hear your mother complaining now: "Why could not you have been a big important truth, like your father?" Being a young proposition, you have not yet made your cut in **B**. You want to make just the right cut, and you do not want to leave anything to chance. You want to make sure you are true. What should you do?

The smart move would be to cut all along the edge of the ellipse that divides **W** from the land of logical chaos. You shade in the entire ellipse. Every world then belongs to your M. Your truth is guaranteed. You will be a logically necessary proposition.

Did I say "a logically necessary proposition"? I meant "the logically necessary proposition." The cut you have made in **B** is not just a way of guaranteeing a proposition's truth, it is the only way. Once you make that cut, no other proposition will be able to follow suit. No other proposition can duplicate your stunning achievement. True, many statements may make the same cut. However, according to our definitions, all statements making a given cut belong to the same proposition. It follows that there can be only one proposition per cut. Your cut is thus unique to you. You get the copyright on it. All statements making that cut will have to belong to you.

"Wait a minute," says your little brother. "Can't I become a necessary proposition too? Here is how I will do it. I will cut a circle out of **B** whose diameter equals the length of my older brother's ellipse. His ellipse and my circle will intersect at two points, namely, the two end points of the ellipse. My circle will thus contain his ellipse, plus a chunk of that incoherent realm you mentioned. I will be necessary, since W_r has to be somewhere inside my cut, but I will not be duplicating my brother's efforts. I will have a cut all my own. Someday my offspring will become logical necessities themselves. All they need to do is draw bigger and bigger circles. As long as each circle contains the ellipse, the kids will do just fine."

I am afraid your little brother is mistaken. He did not pay enough attention to our definitions. Ms and Ns are classes of worlds. A cut is basically a way of assigning possible worlds to Ms and Ns. The space outside the ellipse does not contain any worlds, so the points out there do not belong to either the M or N of any proposition. A proposition cannot do any of its cutting out in logical chaos.

Think of each proposition as cutting **B** with a logical "knife." The knife a proposition wields is tethered to the two foci of the ellipse, W_r and W_θ, with a loop of string. The length of the string is the same for every proposition, and is equal to double the distance between a focus and the point on the ellipse furthest away from that focus.

The defining property of an ellipse is that if you pick any point on the ellipse, the sum of the distances between that point and each of the two foci is a constant. If you hammered two nails into a board, looped a piece of string around the nails, and then pulled the string taut with a pencil, you could use the pencil to draw an ellipse on the board. An ellipse is the only thing you can draw, if you keep the string taut.

Every proposition finds itself in a similar situation. If a proposition pulls its knife across the plane of being until its "string" is taut, the knife only reaches as far as the edge of **W**'s ellipse. No matter what direction the knife goes, the edge of the ellipse represents the limit. But the string does not have to be taut when a proposition makes its cut. Propositions are permitted to cut with the string loose. A proposition can thus cut anywhere inside the ellipse it pleases. Cutting outside the ellipse, however, is forbidden.

So do not listen to your brother. He cannot draw the circle he described. He is just jealous, now that you have become such a big shot among propositions. Being the one and only logically necessary proposition makes you a pretty important fellow. We need to give you a name. Let us dub thee P^λ. Your M encompasses the entire contents of the ellipse. $M[P^\lambda] = \mathbf{W}$, the class of all possible worlds. There is nothing left over to put in your N. $N[P^\lambda]$ has no members. It is the null class.

There is another proposition, not-P^λ, whose M is the null class, and whose N is $\mathbf{W}$. Not-P^λ is the black sheep in your family. His M got your M's leftovers, which is to say, it got nothing. No one wants to be seen talking to that guy. He is guaranteed to be false. No matter what world is the real world, not-$P\lambda$ is not the case.

You might think that P^λ and not-P^λ make the same cut in $\mathbf{B}$. P^λ pulls its knife around the arc formed by the boundary between $\mathbf{W}$ and logical chaos. It assigns all points in $\mathbf{W}$ to M, the rest to N. No worlds fall within N, so N is just the null class. Not-P^λ may be viewed as pulling its knife the same way, along the boundary between order and chaos. Even so, the cuts are different, because the assignment of worlds to Ms and Ns is different. Again, one must pay close attention to the definitions provided. A line contains points, a cut does not. A cut merely divides the class of points $\mathbf{W}$ into two sub-classes, M and N. If the M and N are different, then so is the cut. The Ms and Ns of P^λ and not-P^λ are reversed. The M of one is the N of the other. The cuts these propositions make are thus also the reversals of one another.

One can also see not-P^λ as the only proposition that makes no use of its knife. It represents the limiting case in which the collection of worlds within M shrinks until it vanishes altogether. So the knife never has to touch the plane. It is like cutting a pie into one piece (we do not need a knife to do that). Still, in our technical sense of "cut," not-P^λ does make a cut, since it assigns all worlds to either its M or its N. It is a knife-less cut. It is, moreover, the same cut, whether we imagine the knife being drawn along the boundary mentioned, or being left in the kitchen drawer.

If not-P^λ can cut **B** without actually putting the knife to the plane, so other propositions may cut **B** by slicing into it multiple times. Consider some proposition P such that P is equivalent to "either Q or R." M[P] will in that case be the union of M[Q] and M[R]. M[Q] and M[R], however, could well represent discrete, nonintersecting chunks of **B**. M[P] will then consist of two unconnected parts. Technically speaking, P cuts **B** just once, even though it has to put its knife in **B** twice. There is no limit to the number of "slices" that may go into a cut. There may be two, or ten, or a hundred. A map of M[P], shaded against the background provided by **B**, could look like the map of some island archipelago with a background of ocean.

15

What statements express P^λ? Tautologies always do. Consider the statement, "All tall men are tall." This has to be true. The statement does not claim that there are any tall men. It merely claims that all the tall men there are, are tall. According to the conventions of logic, this would be a fair claim, even if there were no tall men. In fact, there do not have to be men of any kind. All tall men are tall, even in $\mathbf{W}_0$. A similar analysis could be done on any tautology. Tautologies leave nothing to chance. They provide no hostages to fortune. Each tautology guarantees its own truth by relying solely on definitions and logical conventions. Every tautology is thus a necessary truth, and an instance of P^λ.

Statements of logical rules also express P^λ. "If A = B, and B = C, then A = C" expresses P^λ, as does this statement: "If P implies Q, then P implies not-not-Q."

Self-evident truths fall under P^λ's umbrella as well. Examples of this might include the following: "The whole is greater than the part," "No object can be in two places at once," and, "Nothing can be both black and white and also red all over." In the *Declaration of Independence*, Thomas Jefferson claimed that all men are created equal, and that they are endowed by their Creator with certain inalienable rights. He also claimed that these facts were self-evident. I feel inclined to agree that men are, in some sense, equal, and that they do possess certain rights. Are these facts self-evident? Perhaps. But the fact that they are self-evident is not itself self-evident, at least not to me.

All the truths of pure mathematics express P^λ. Two plus two is four in every conceivable world. The world does not have to contain two of anything, or four of anything, in order for S(3) to be true. Just as all tall men are tall, even in a world deprived of men, so two plus two is four, even in a world bereft of couples and quartets. Similar reasoning applies to S(3)', the statement regarding imaginary numbers. $2\sqrt{-1} + 2\sqrt{-1} = 4\sqrt{-1}$, even if the world contains no piles of apples containing four times the square root of negative one apples.

We can take this view of mathematical truths without assuming all such truths to be tautologies. Given any mathematical system, such as Euclidean geometry, there may well be some truths in the system that we cannot deduce from the definitions and axioms of that system. Truths of that sort would not be tautologies, but they would still be necessary truths, and hence, instances of P^λ.

The huge variety of statements occurring within P^λ should put to rest the idea that statements are equivalent if and only if they "mean the same thing." By the definition of "equivalent" given earlier, all necessary truths are equivalent. They all have the same M, so they are all true for the same class of possible worlds. Consequently, they all express a single proposition. Yet clearly they do not all "mean the same thing." "Two plus two equals four" does not mean what is meant by "the sum of the angles in a triangle is equal to two right angles." In no sense could either statement serve as a translation for the other. According to any ordinary understanding of the word "fact," the two statements do not relate the same fact. This, however, does not falsify the claim that they express the same proposition.

The members of a proposition always constitute a natural class. They have something important in common: they all make the same cut. In other respects, the membership of a proposition may be as diverse as you please. A mind-boggling variety may lie atop that underlying unity. If nothing else, P^λ shows just how mind-boggling the variety can be.

It would seem, though, that if two statements do "mean the same thing," so that either could be considered a translation for the other, then they would express the same proposition. A translation of S(1) into French or German should not alter the proposition being expressed. A translation that did alter the proposition in any significant manner would simply be a bad translation.[12]

16

Statements that assert existence never belong to P^λ. The presence of $\mathbf{W}_\varnothing$ in $\mathbf{B}$ creates an obstacle to membership in P^λ that no positive existential claim can surmount. Nothing exists in $\mathbf{W}_\varnothing$, so any statement that asserts existence cannot be true of $\mathbf{W}_\varnothing$. But if a statement is not true of that world, then it is not true of all possible worlds. Hence, it cannot be a necessary truth. It cannot express P^λ.

The famous ontological proof of the existence of God attempts to hurdle this barrier. The proof defines God as the being greater than which no being can be conceived. The idea here is not that God is the greatest conceivable being, but rather that God is inconceivably great. However, the logic of the proof remains the same, whichever view of God we take. Having defined God in this manner, the proof goes on to assert the incoherence of supposing God not to exist. "We cannot conceive of God as not existing," the proof says. "For if we did, we could then conceive of a being greater than God, namely, a being that had all of God's attributes, plus existence, and that would be contrary to our definition, which plainly states that nothing greater than God may be conceived."

The proof is very clever. If we start from the premise that God is supremely great, we must accept that God has all the attributes of such greatness: omnipotence, omniscience, perfect virtue, and so on. It is then tempting to add existence to the list. Wouldn't a real God be greater than a merely fictitious one? A God who exists must have infinitely more power than one who does not. Hence, the concept of God must include the concept of existence. Once this is understood, it becomes impossible to conceive of God as not existing. One must believe that he exists. He cannot fail to exist—or so the proof would have us think.

There is nothing wrong with the proof's definition of God. It makes perfect sense to define God as the being of unsurpassable greatness, the being whose greatness exceeds the limits of human conception. The God of the ontological proof does not have as much personality as the God of the Old Testament. Still, the definition does capture an important aspect of the God concept. To most of us, including those of us who are atheists, a God any smaller than the definition calls for would not be God.

One might question the propriety of counting existence as a mark of greatness. Is a real God greater than a fictitious God? If so, then a real anthill must be bigger than an imaginary mountain. It seems odd to compare real things with unreal ones. It is not as if we could put a real midget next to an imaginary basketball player to see who is taller. However, for the sake of argument, let us accept the convention that the real is superior to the unreal in terms of greatness, height, or whatever measure seems most relevant. If we accept this convention and the definition of God provided, are we then compelled to accept the ontological proof's conclusion?

No. Definitions, like statements, have logical forms. Not all definitions have the same form. There can be different forms for different purposes. We would not define an individual the same way we would a class. We could not define games or bears the way we might gold. However, no definition asserts the existence of the thing defined. If it does, then it is not a definition. It is a statement about that thing. Definitions and statements are logically distinct items. A definition cannot also be a statement, any more than a dog can do double duty as a cat.

The given definition of God has a logical form something like this: "For any x, if x has the property p, then x is y." Fleshing out the form, we get this: "For any x, if x is the being greater than which no being can be conceived, then x is God." Putting the definition in the right form makes it clear what the definition can and cannot do. The definition does not claim that there is any such being as the one it identifies. It merely states that if there were such a being, then that being would be God. So let the marks of supreme greatness be omnipotence, omniscience, and perfect virtue. A being with all those wonderful qualities would be God, but it does not follow that there is a God. We can make existence one of the marks of greatness if you like. A being would then have to exist, and be omnipotent, omniscient, and so forth, in order to count as God. But it is a superfluous addition. When we employ the phrase "for any x," we are already taking it for granted that the X's under consideration are real things. If a given x is not real, then the question "Is it y?" does not arise. If we found a real piece of yellow rock, we might want to know if it was gold or iron pyrite. We are never going to find a fictitious rock, so we will never bother to ask if it is fictitious gold.

The proof thus loses all plausibility when we put it in proper form. Its cover is blown, it ceases to look clever. The proof confuses definitions with statements. It offers a definition of God, but expects us to grant that definition the logical force of a statement. Now, of course, once we accept the statement that God is inconceivably great, we must accept that God is. The statement does imply that. But in accepting the proof's definition, we in no way commit ourselves to that statement. The definition does not commit us to anything except a linguistic convention. In accepting the definition, we agree that should we encounter a being of sufficient greatness, we will call that being "God." Nothing more is involved. Nothing of any existential import follows from the definition.

The ontological proof also misconceives the concept of conception. The proof holds that we cannot conceive of a nonexistent God. We can only conceive of him as existing. Hence, he must exist. But conceiving and believing are separate things. We can conceive of God as existing and still not believe that God exists, for even if the concept of God includes existence as one of God's attributes, it is still legitimate to ask whether that concept has any application. The concept alone cannot guarantee that any real entity corresponds to it. Grasping the concept does not get us outside our own heads. It does not give us any information concerning the world's contents.

If one is tempted to make existence a mark of greatness, then one may also wish to put necessary existence on the list of divine qualities. A God who existed necessarily might be thought greater than one who simply happened to be. A logically contingent God would be either a kind of cosmic accident, or else dependent for his existence on something outside himself. Either alternative would appear to impugn God's dignity. To safeguard that dignity, one might postulate that God must possess the reason for his existence within himself. His existence must emerge out of the very nature of existence itself. But even God cannot accomplish the logically impossible. He cannot make two plus two equal five. I have no idea what it would mean to say this, but let us say that God does possess within himself the reason for his own existence. He is, in some sense, self-caused. So he is not an accident, nor in any way dependent. Even then, it would not be the case that God existed in every conceivable world. For example, he would still not exist in $W_{\o}$. God may have omnipotent sway over reality, but he has no such power over the realm of the merely possible. He cannot put copies of himself in other worlds. But if self-caused Gods do not rule in all possible worlds, then God is not, in the sense used here, logically necessary. The statement maintaining that he exists does not express P^{λ}. And neither does any other positive existential claim.

17

Mathematical truths all express P^{λ}. How can this be? In Euclidean geometry, parallel lines never meet. In other geometries they do. In Euclidean geometry, the angles of a triangle always add up to two right angles. In other geometries they often do not. So how can Euclid's statement concerning the angles of a triangle be equivalent to a rival geometry's statement on the same issue? It seems absurd to suppose that contradictory statements could express the same proposition. Two incompatible statements cannot both be true. Either one statement is true and the other is false, or neither is true. If we take the first view, we end up treating mathematical systems as if they were hypotheses in physics, and we have to examine physical space to see if it is Euclidean or non-Euclidean. If we take the second view, then we effectively banish truth from mathematics. The term "mathematical truth" becomes an oxymoron.

The analysis of apparently contradictory mathematical statements follows the model we used to analyze the apparently contradictory statements issued by scientific observers working in different frames of reference. To review, let there be two observers watching the movements of a ship. One observer claims the ship is moving, the other says it is stationary. The observers appear to contradict one another, yet both may be speaking correctly. Observer A claims the ship is moving, meaning that is moving through his frame of reference. This claim is compatible with B's assertion that the ship is stationary, which it is, relative to B's referential frame.

The observers of the ship are expressing different, but compatible, propositions. The Euclidean geometer and his non-Euclidean colleague are relating different, but compatible, facts falling under the umbrella of a single proposition. That the angles of a triangle add up to two right angles is true in Euclidean geometry. Within the context of that conceptual frame of reference, it is a perfectly appropriate thing to say. Likewise, the non-Euclidean geometer speaks correctly if he says that the angles add up to something else. They do add up to something else, within the frame of reference provided by that geometer's definitions and axioms. The definitions and axioms of each system are neither true nor false. They simply create the conceptual frameworks within which geometers operate.

In the example of the ship, observers A and B are both stating objective facts. The ship's motion may be relative, but the truth values of the propositions A and B express are not. The proposition A expresses about the ship is absolutely true. It is true for him, true for B, and true for everybody else as well. The same goes for the proposition B expresses. With regard to geometry, the Euclidean and non-Euclidean geometers are also both stating objective facts. It is a plain matter of fact that the angles of every triangle in a Euclidean space add up to two right angles. It is equally true to assert that in non-Euclidean spaces, the angles generally add up to something else. These are objective facts concerning, respectively, Euclidean and non-Euclidean spaces. The facts have little relation to one another except that, as mentioned, they fall under the same proposition.

We could also compare the case of the two geometers with that involving Earth and Earth Two. Observers on those different planets sometimes made apparently contradictory statements concerning William and Harold. The appearance of contradiction disappears when we understand that the observers are talking about different sets of men. When Earthlings speak of William, they refer to the William on Earth. When the denizens of Earth Two speak of William, they refer to the completely different fellow who lived on their own planet. Likewise, we might say that the two geometers are simply speaking about and referring to different objects. The Euclidean geometer is discussing the properties of Euclidean spaces, the non-Euclidean geometer those of non-Euclidean spaces. The geometers need not argue over which type of space best represents physical space. That question belongs to physics. As mathematicians, they can afford to be agnostic about whether the world contains any objects like those they describe. The facts these mathematicians relate remain facts, even if there are no such spaces. The Euclidean geometer does not have to claim that there are any Euclidean triangles. Even if none exist, it is still the case that for every such triangle its angles add up to two right angles. The logic of this is the same we employed when we said that all tall men would be tall, even in a world with no tall men.

The existence of different geometrical systems thus in no way compromises the idea that mathematical statements express objective truths.

18

The sample sentence S(1) is, let us assume, true. The sentence also contains $\mathbf{W}_r$ in its M. As noted earlier, S(1) is true because it contains $\mathbf{W}_r$ in its M. The members of M[S(1)] all have an important property in common, namely, the property of containing an event, the Battle of Hastings, wherein William defeats Harold. That $\mathbf{W}_r$ has this property explains why S(1) is true. S(1) is not just true of some class of worlds. It is true of $\mathbf{W}_r$. Hence, it is true absolutely and without qualification.

One might balk at describing S(3) this way. That the title of "$\mathbf{W}_r$" happens to belong to this world, rather than some other, does not appear to explain why S(3) is true. $\mathbf{W}_r$ could have been another world, literally any other world, and S(3)'s truth value would remain unchanged. So it seems that S(3) is not true because it contains $\mathbf{W}_r$ in its M.

On the contrary (and doing my best imitation of Thomas Aquinas here), I say that S(3) really is true because it contains $\mathbf{W}_r$ in its M. The members of M[S(3)] constitute a natural class. They all have something important in common, namely, the property of being coherently conceivable worlds. Because they have this property, all of their quartets can be resolved into pairs of couples. $\mathbf{W}_r$ possesses the property just mentioned, which explains why S(3) is true. If $\mathbf{W}_r$ did not have that property, or if it did not belong to S(3)'s M, then S(3) would be false. With S(3), as with S(1), we may say that it is not just true of some class of worlds. It is true of $\mathbf{W}_r$. Hence, it is true absolutely and without qualification.

Of course, the bar here has been set low, low enough so that all worlds can get over it. We have arranged things to guarantee that all possible worlds are coherently conceivable. We simply make "possible" and "coherently conceivable" convertible terms. The game is thus fixed. However, this does not mean that the pattern of analysis used on S(1) needs any modification to fit S(3). The same pattern will work for both. We just need to realize that S(3) constitutes a limiting case.

The defining property of M[S(1)] is very specific. $\mathbf{W}_r$ has to be a special kind of world to have that particular property. The Ms of many other statements have defining properties that are less specific. For example, suppose we said "William won the Battle of Hastings during the eleventh century." Our statement omits the year in which the event took place, and also leaves out the name of the man William defeated. It is thus less specific. Its M will encompass a much broader collection of worlds. If we said, "William won a battle during the Middle Ages," that statement would have even less specificity, and its M would be broader still.

We could continue this process, constructing statements containing less and less information about the world, statements with increasingly large and diverse Ms: "There are men," "There are living things," "There is at least one material object." Statements such as S(3) stand at the far end of this process. They constitute the limiting cases for which information content has sunk to the minimum, and for which M has expanded to the maximum. Still, our method for analyzing truths can be applied throughout the spectrum of specificity.

One might ask what remains of our basic intuition that truth involves a relation to reality. Truth, we believe, is whatever bears the right relationship to the real world. But mathematical truths are not about reality, so the reader might feel inclined to say that they bear no relation at all to the real world. He could offer the criticism that containment theory is trying to manufacture a relation where none exists.

I do not believe this to be a fair criticism. The field of mathematics does relate to the real world. Moreover, its relationship to reality is of the right kind for it to count as a body of truths. How else can we explain the utility of mathematics in all the sciences? It possesses enormous descriptive and explanatory power precisely because it does relate to reality "in the right way." Its power derives from the fact that it relates to every conceivable world in exactly the same way. The principles of mathematics are thus guaranteed to work no matter what world turns out to be the real one.

19

The reader may still feel that I have tried too hard to amalgamate mathematical with historical and scientific statements. Like the person Wittgenstein described, who was too eager to define "tool," I may have been too eager to define "truth." In my eagerness I may have papered over some distinctions that ought not to be ignored. I plead guilty. I did gloss over an important distinction between S(1) and S(3). I need to correct that oversight.

We should distinguish between what causes a statement, and what causes it to be true. Think again of S(1). Cutting **B** in a particular way is S(1)'s logical function. Achieving that cut is part of S(1)'s purpose, and thus part of its final cause. You might say that making the cut is S(1)'s *raison d'être*. As noted before, this reason is not necessarily a reason in anyone's mind. S(1)'s speaker does not have to think about the cut. He does not even have to know what cuts are. It is a logical, not psychological, reason. Daniel Dennett would call it a "free-floating rationale." Dennett employed the concept in the context of evolutionary theory to explain how the features of a species can evolve for a purpose, even though it is not a purpose in anyone's mind. The purpose is instead built into the process of natural selection.[13] We can employ the concept here, and say that cutting **B** in a specific manner is S(1)'s free-floating rationale. The rationale is built into S(1)'s logical nature.

S(1)'s cut "causes" the statement by constituting its final cause. But what causes the statement to be true? Reality does. S(1) is true because it describes a real event, and because the real world, $\mathbf{W}_r$, has the properties S(1) assigns to it. Reality, we might say, is the efficient cause of S(1)'s truth.

Let us return to S(3). Like S(1), S(3) performs the logical function of cutting **B** into an M and an N. Making this cut provides the free floating rationale for S(3)'s existence. Like S(1), S(3) is true because it contains $\mathbf{W}_r$ in its M. This is the cause of the statement's truth. The analogy between S(1) and S(3) seems complete.

Some readers may sense a key disanalogy between the two statements. Reality makes a plausible efficient cause for S(1)'s truth. A similar claim for S(3)'s truth seems far less plausible. In fact, with respect to S(3)'s truth value, reality might seem irrelevant. S(3) is true no matter what reality is like. Logic, not reality, appears to be the efficient cause of S(3)'s truth. So while S(3) is true, and contains $\mathbf{W}_r$ in its M, the latter fact about S(3) does not explain the former. But using the latter to explain the former is what containment theory is all about. The viability of the theory appears threatened.

We can rescue containment theory by focusing attention on the material, not the efficient, causes of truth. We still view reality as the efficient cause of truth for historical and scientific statements. We also admit that this is not the case for mathematical statements. The efficient causes of truth for mathematical statements are instead the definitions and axioms of the deductive systems in which those statements appear. S(3), for example, derives its truth from the definitions and axioms embedded in arithmetic. However, we now add the idea that the material cause for any statement's truth lies in the fact that P^n entails it. For any truth S, the syllogism, "If P^n, then S" constitutes S's truth because that syllogism is what places $\mathbf{W}_r$ inside M[S]. Syllogisms of that sort are how Ms are constructed. By definition, whatever constitutes a thing is its material cause. "If P^n, then S" is thus the material cause of S's truth, and this relationship holds true no matter what type of statement S is. S may be historical, scientific, or mathematical. On this interpretation, S(3) is true because it contains $\mathbf{W}_r$ in its M. However, the "because" in this statement should be taken to refer to a material cause. The material cause of truth is always the same, no matter how large a statement's M might be. It remains the same, even in the limiting case where the M is all-encompassing.

"Why does S(3) need a material cause of truth?" the reader might ask. "If S(3) has an efficient cause, i.e., the definitions and axioms of arithmetic, then that should suffice to make it true. Adding a material cause to the mix seems superfluous." But the definitions and axioms of arithmetic do not by themselves suffice to make S(3) true. As we noted during our discussion of the ontological proof for the existence of God, definitions are neither true nor false. They have no truth values. The same may be said of axioms. Taken by themselves, they are assumptions, not truths. But when we deduce a conclusion from an assumption, we can only preserve a truth value already present. To say that a conclusion C follows from some assumption A is merely to say that if A is true, then C is also true. If it has a positive truth value, A transmits that to C. Yet the definitions and axioms of arithmetic have no truth values. Hence, they have nothing to transmit to conclusions such as S(3).

We need to add that connection to reality, which is what containment theory accomplishes.

20

The reader is still unhappy, I can tell. "Of course P^n entails S(3)," the reader might say. "But so what? Every other proposition does exactly the same thing!" The reader is correct. It is a theorem of containment theory that for any two propositions P and Q, P entails Q if and only if M[P] is a subset of M[Q].[14] Think about this for a moment and you will see why the theorem works. If P is true, then $\mathbf{W}_r$ falls within its M. But if $\mathbf{W}_r$ falls within that M, it will also fall within Q's M, if Q's M contains P's. Thus, if P is true, Q must be true also, since both will contain $\mathbf{W}_r$ in their Ms. S(3) expresses the proposition P^λ, whose M is identical with $\mathbf{W}$, the class of all conceivable worlds. M[P^λ] contains every other conceivable M. Every other M is its subset. So every proposition without exception entails P^λ. If they entail P^λ, then they also entail all of P^λ's instances, including S(3).

P^n is thus hardly unique in its entailment of S(3). However, the syllogism, "If P^n, then S(3)" remains, in a sense, uniquely valuable. It is the one syllogism that links S(3) to reality. The position of containment theory is that the extreme generality of P^λ and its instances does not make their truth independent of reality, at least not completely. Even though P^λ would be true for any world, we are entitled to call it true (without qualification) only because it is true for this world, the real one. That connection with reality is still what makes P^λ true. In technical terms, the connection to reality constitutes the material cause of P^λ's truth. The same holds for all of P^λ's instances, S(3) included.

Here are two corollaries to our theorem. First, every proposition entails itself (because every M is a subclass of itself). Second, the proposition not-P^λ entails every other proposition, including, paradoxically, P^λ. The M of not-P^λ is the null class, which is a subset of every other class.

21

The world is full of objects. These objects have dispositions. We know this as surely as we know that there are objects. Yet dispositions might be thought rather peculiar. Unlike objects, they are not part of the world's furniture. The dispositions of objects are not themselves objects. If we look for them "out there" in the world, we cannot find them.

Think of a cube of sugar. Put it in a cup of hot coffee and it dissolves. That the cube dissolves is no accident. Nothing miraculous is happening. The cube merely has a disposition to dissolve. It is, in other words, soluble. Dissolving in substances like hot coffee is what any normal sugar cube would do. It is what we quite rationally expect sugar cubes to do.

But where is the sugar cube's disposition to dissolve? It is not a part of the cube. We can cut open a frog in biology class and find its heart, its liver, and its lungs. We cannot in any comparable fashion cut open a sugar cube and find its solubility. The problem here is not one of technology. It is not as if we might find the solubility if we just had a more powerful microscope. The problem has to do with logic. Dispositions (like solubility) and objects (like hearts and livers) are not the same kinds of things. They belong to different logical types.

"Wait a minute," you might say. "We can find the sugar's solubility using instruments such as microscopes. Those instruments allow us to discover the sugar's molecular structure, which explains why the cube dissolves the way it does." I agree. The molecular structure does explain the sugar's solubility. Yet it is not identical to that solubility. There remains a crucial logical distinction between the structure and the disposition. The "structure" of the sugar refers to the way the sugar's atomic parts are arranged. The sugar's "disposition" refers to its behavioral tendencies—to the way the sugar does behave, as well as to how it would (under various contra-factual conditions) behave. Objects can have the same disposition without having the same structure. Lots of substances are soluble besides sugar. Of course, anything with sugar's structure will also have sugar's dispositions. If it is structured like sugar, then it is sugar, so of course it will act like sugar. But we can certainly imagine worlds where sugar is not soluble. The molecular structure would be the same, but the behavioral properties would be different. Perhaps, in such worlds, sugar cubes do not dissolve in hot coffee. They vibrate, turn into salt, or explode. Do not say "That's impossible." Of course it is impossible—in this world. In other worlds it might be a different story.

To say of the sugar that it has a certain molecular structure is thus not equivalent to saying that it is soluble. Those are different propositions. The molecular structure cannot be the solubility, even if it explains the solubility. In finding the former, we have not found the latter.

The dispositions of material objects are not themselves the material objects. Does that make them immaterial objects? No. Dispositions are not objects at all. Even if we imagined dispositions to be ghostly entities lurking within objects, that would not solve the problem at hand. It would only recreate the problem on another level, for the ghostly entities would themselves have dispositions. They would tend to behave in certain ways, but not others. So what would those dispositions be? Are they objects too? Must we postulate ghosts inside the ghosts, and further ghosts inside the ghosts of the ghosts? That will not work, and we should not bother trying to make it work. It is far better to admit that dispositions belong to a different logical type than objects. They cannot be equated either with objects, or with structures of objects. Dispositions enjoy a unique ontological status.

22

How should we interpret statements about dispositions? In referring to a disposition, we are not referring to an object or a structure, but to the actual and potential behavior of whatever thing is said to possess that disposition. It is easy to get a grip on actual behavior, which consists of real events "out there," in the real world. But what can we make of "potential" behavior? What does it mean to refer to that? If behavior is merely potential, then it is not actual. If we look "out there," we will not find it. So where is it?

For containment theory, the answer is clear. If the behavior is not happening in this world, then it must be placed in some other world. The merely potential actions of the actual world are the actualized events of merely potential worlds. This is the whole function of potential, or rather, of possible, worlds. Possible worlds are the logical fictions we create in order to have a place to put all the things that do not exist, together with all the events that do not happen.

It follows that statements concerning dispositions refer, in part, to other worlds. This distinguishes such statements from purely historical statements like S(1). S(1) referred to this world, and only to this one. William, Harold, the epic battle between them—it is all right here in $\mathbf{W}_r$. But a statement along the lines of, "This cube of sugar is soluble," refers to events beyond $\mathbf{W}_r$'s confines. These events, the hypothetical consequences of contrafactual conditions, constitute the contents of worlds similar to, but not quite identical to, $\mathbf{W}_r$. We may think of worlds like this as occupying points close to $\mathbf{W}_r$'s in the plane of being. They are $\mathbf{W}_r$'s "neighbors."

In our eagerness to discuss mathematical statements such as S(3), we inadvertently skipped over S(2). S(2) concerns a law of nature, which makes it a statement about dispositions. S(2) tells us how physical objects can be expected to behave. The law it expresses is meant to cover not only how bodies do behave, but how they have behaved in the past, how they will behave in the future, and also how they would behave under a large variety of contra-factual conditions. In short, S(2) identifies a disposition possessed by every material thing.

Like other dispositional statements, S(2) refers to an indefinitely large array of events that are merely potential. These potential events occur only in the fictional worlds of our imagination, the worlds that constitute the logical construct we call **B**. The same may be said of other statements of natural law, and of many other law-like utterances. They refer not just to the contents of this world, but to the contents of this world's neighbors in imaginary space.

23

Since **B** is merely a logical construct, not a real thing, you might think it arbitrary which worlds get designated as "neighbors." Can't we arrange worlds on the plane of being any way we please? Where on the map a world goes would seem to be a matter of our whim. But if that is the case, then what force is there to the claim that law-like statements refer in part to W_r's "neighbors?"

Think of the class that contains all living things. This is a real class with real members. Still, it would appear to be up to us how we want to divide this class into subclasses. We could start by grouping them according to color. Yellow creatures would go in one group, blue ones in another. Within each color group we could arrange organisms by weight. Each weight class would then be subdivided according to an organism's utility. Creatures that taste good would go in one pile, those used for medical purposes in another. But of course we don't do anything this ridiculous. We use the Linnaean system of classification. Plants are divided from animals, reptiles from mammals, mammals with paws from mammals with hooves, and so on. We do not put the whales in with the fish, even though whales and fish both live in the sea. We put the whales with the mammals. Doing things this way does not seem arbitrary. We feel that we are, in some perfectly appropriate sense, "dividing nature at the joints." We are, in short, discovering how life on Earth is in fact organized.

Something like this is the case with respect to the membership of **W**. Some ways of arranging and classifying worlds make more sense than others. Some ways may do a better job than others of revealing **B**'s fundamental logical structure. Although **B** may be just a logical construct, the same might be said of Euclidean geometry. Yet figures in Euclidean spaces can have properties we do not assign to them. The definitions and axioms of Euclidean geometry are ours to select, but having made our choice about those things, the rest is not up to us. We cannot pick and choose which theorems we want to be true, and which we would prefer to be false. The truth or falsity of any theorem is a matter of logic, not whim.

Suppose we specify, as an axiom of containment theory, that the members of **W** should be deployed across **B** according to similarity, and that deeper, more fundamental similarities should take priority over relatively superficial ones. With that axiom in place, things are no longer entirely up to us. The arrangement of worlds in the plane is not just a matter of whim. The distinction between deep and superficial resemblances is not arbitrary. That a mammal with green fur has more in common with other mammals than it does with green plants, is not a matter of taste or opinion. It is a fact. It can be equally factual to say of some given pair of worlds that they have more in common with each other than they do with worlds of another type.

24

So far we have spoken of **B** as if it were an undifferentiated plane. Why not add some color to it? Picture a political map of Europe. There are dozens of countries of different sizes and shapes, each marked on the map by a different color. France is in red, Italy in yellow, Great Britain blue. Now imagine a "political" map of **B**. Each "country" on the map appears in a different color. What distinguishes one country from another? In Europe, each country has its own laws. To go from one nation to another is to go from one legal jurisdiction to another. Let it be the same in **B**. The "countries" in **B** are sets of worlds such that all worlds within any given set obey the same group of natural laws. A country in **B** is a region in the plane of being where a given bundle of natural laws holds sway.

Of course, there is only a vague analogy between natural laws and the laws passed by national legislatures. Natural laws and human laws are about as much alike as grizzly bears and Chicago Bears." Yet the legal system of a world still represents that world's most fundamental feature. It is the unity underlying the world's plurality. So, if worlds are going to be arranged in the plane of being according to deep similarities, similarity of laws must take priority. Worlds will be grouped first and foremost by the laws they obey. Worlds obeying the same laws will form countries. Countries with similar laws will form leagues and continents.

Now return to S(2). As a statement of natural law, S(2) refers not just to events in $\mathbf{W}_r$ but to countless events we can imagine occurring elsewhere in the country where $\mathbf{W}_r$ resides. No doubt there is an entire continent in **B** full of countries where the natural law identified by S(2) is in force. The M of S(2) contains all the worlds located on that continent. S(2) is true if $\mathbf{W}_r$ is on the continent S(2) has identified. Otherwise S(2) is false. The analysis of Ms, Ns, and truth values is pretty much the same for S(2) as it was for S(1) and S(3).

Where these statements differ is in the size of their Ms and the extent of their reference. S(1) is true of a class of worlds, roughly the class containing battles at Hastings wherein William defeats Harold. But S(1) only refers to the contents of this world. Its whole concern is with the real battle that took place in 1066. S(2) has a larger M, and its reference is also greater, since it refers to events outside of $\mathbf{W}_r$. S(3) enjoys the largest M of all, since it contains all possible worlds. One is tempted to say that S(3) also enjoys the greatest reference, since it refers to all the couples and quartets to be found anywhere in **W**. Yet it might be better to say that S(3) makes no reference to anything. S(3) is not "about" couples and quartets, at least not in the way that S(1) is "about" the Battle of Hastings. Lack of reference is precisely what makes a statement of pure mathematics such as S(3) "pure."

25

One might ask, "Does W_r reside in a particular country because it obeys the laws of that country, or does it obey those laws because it resides there?" This might at first seem like a foolish question, on a par with asking whether we laugh at jokes because they are funny, or whether they are funny because they make us laugh. On second thought, the answer appears obvious: W_r and its fellow citizens get placed together in one country because they all obey the same laws. Adherence to that legal system is the criterion for citizenship. Things are not quite that simple, however. We need to give the issue a third look.

Think of an atom of gold. What makes that atom a gold atom, not an atom of some other element? The seventy-nine protons in the atom's nucleus are what make it gold. If its nucleus contained a different number of protons, then the atom would be a different element. This is just a matter of definition. What makes the atom gold is internal to the atom, so the property of being gold is an internal property.

Think of the property of being someone's father. Is this also an internal property? Clearly it is not. Looking only inside a man, we could not tell for sure whose father he was, or even if he was anyone's father. He might believe himself to be the father of a particular boy, but that, by itself, would prove nothing. What if a DNA test revealed that he had the right genes to be the boy's father? The test would not be decisive; he might be the father's twin brother. Besides, in conducting the test in comparing the DNA samples, we would be using information about the boy; and that is information external to the man in question. Being someone's father involves more than being in the right physical or mental state. It is not just a matter of thinking certain thoughts, or having one's molecules arranged in the right pattern. Being a father depends upon many factors external to the father himself. There must also be a child and a mother, and a history of events connecting those individuals to the man. This makes fatherhood an external property.

Now reconsider the solubility of the sugar cube. What makes the sugar soluble? In one sense of "make," we could say that it is the sugar's molecular structure that makes it soluble. Having that structure causes the sugar to be soluble. The structure explains the solubility. In the sense of "make" relevant here, though, the molecular structure is not what makes the sugar soluble. The structure does not constitute the solubility. We do not define "solubility" in terms of having a specific molecular structure, the way we define gold as having a specific nuclear content. As mentioned before, if we look for the solubility inside the sugar, we will not find it. Nothing internal to the sugar cube constitutes its solubility. Solubility is not an internal property.

If solubility is not an internal property, then it must be an external property. Those are our only two choices. Yet the sugar's solubility does not depend on its history, the way a man's fatherhood depends on his history. The sugar cube can be soluble without ever having actually dissolved in anything. Indeed, the cube could not have displayed its solubility at any time in the past. If it had, it would not still be a cube. The sugar's solubility is also independent of the sugar's relations to real objects. There has to be a real son "out there" in the world, and a real mother too, in order for a man to be a father. But the sugar can be soluble, even if there are no cups of hot coffee for it to dissolve in. So, if we look for the sugar's solubility outside the sugar, we still cannot find it, at least not if we confine our search to $\mathbf{W}_r$.

So where is the sugar's solubility? We should already know the answer to that. To say that the cube of sugar is soluble is to say that it would dissolve if placed in a suitable medium. What constitutes the solubility is thus a set of hypothetical events, most or all of which will never happen. To put it another way, what constitutes the sugar's solubility is the sugar's relation to events that occur only in fictional worlds.

What we have said concerning solubility applies also to other dispositions. Dispositional properties are external properties. Whether a given entity possesses a given disposition depends on how that entity relates to other worlds.

We are ready to return to the question regarding natural laws. We know that events in the real world obey certain natural laws. $\mathbf{W}_r$, we might say, is disposed to obey those laws. But this dispositional property, which $\mathbf{W}_r$ indubitably possesses, is not something internal to it. Like other dispositional properties, it is external. It depends on the connecting links between $\mathbf{W}_r$ and other, fictional worlds. So if we ask, "Does $\mathbf{W}_r$ reside in a particular country because it obeys the laws of that country, or does it obey those laws because it resides there?" the answer is an emphatic "Yes." We specified that worlds should be grouped according to the laws they obey. W_r obeys a certain set of laws, so on our map of the plane of being, it gets placed in the country where those laws hold sway. But W_r is only subject to those laws because it has the neighbors it does. W_r's subjection to those laws is determined by the connecting links between W_r and those neighbors. These links are not up to us. We do not make them what they are, even though the plane of being is our creation, our construct. This is a surpassingly strange thing to say, but it is true.

26

We turn next to the interpretation of moral statements. Allow me to begin with my conclusion: moral statements, if they are true, express P^λ. If false, they express not-P^λ. This idea is plausible when the statement in question is something like, "Patience is a virtue." The truth of such a statement is a function of the meanings of the words employed. Patience is virtuous by definition. We would not describe someone as "patient" if we thought he or she was doing the wrong thing. We might say that they were engaged in wishful thinking (because in our view they are waiting for an event that will never happen), or that they are procrastinators (putting off some action that needs to be done immediately). "Patience is a virtue," then, would appear to be a tautology, on a par with saying that all fathers are men, or that every champion is a winner. As is the case with any tautology, it belongs to P^λ.

The statement S(4), if true, would also express P^λ. If rape is morally wrong, then it is always wrong. It is wrong in all possible worlds. But suppose we said, "Men ought not to rape women." Our statement appears to presuppose the existence of both men and women. Should it then be considered false of worlds where people are absent? I do not believe so. Even in an uninhabited world, it would still be the case that men ought not to rape women. The logic here is the same we used when we claimed that two plus two would be four, even in a world without couples or quartets.

What about moral statements that refer directly to real individuals, actions, or states of affairs? Consider a statement like, "John is a virtuous man." Does the truth of this depend on there being a man named John? Yes it does, which is why I would not consider it a moral statement. The use of a moral term does not make a statement a moral statement, any more than the use of a number word makes a statement mathematical. "There are five apples on the table" is not a mathematical statement, at least not in the sense employed here. Whether there are five apples on the table, or two, or none, is a matter of historical fact. "There are five apples on the table" has more in common with S(1) than it does with S(3). Similarly, the statement "John is a virtuous man" is either a biographical fact about John, or else someone's opinion of John. It is not, strictly speaking, a moral statement.

But we are assuming that moral statements can have truth values. This is a big assumption. One might well feel that when we make moral statements, we leave the realm of fact and enter the realm of value. In the realm of value, does the concept of truth even apply? Everything there may be a matter of opinion. So one could question whether the concept of "moral truth" even makes sense. We thus need to give some account of how moral truth is possible. We need to link moral truths to the other kinds of truths already discussed. We also need to defend the claim that moral truths enjoy the same logical status as mathematical truths, which seems to be implied by the idea that mathematical and moral truths all express the same proposition, namely P^{λ}.[15]

27

Before going any further I want to quote a passage written by one of my masters, C. S. Lewis. The passage is from the opening pages of *Mere Christianity*:

Every one has heard people quarrelling. Sometimes it sounds funny and sometimes it sounds merely unpleasant; but however it sounds, I believe we can learn something very important from listening to the kinds of things they say. They say things like this: "How'd you like it if anyone did the same to you?" – "That's my seat; I was there first!" – "Leave him alone, he is not doing you any harm." —"Why should you shove in first?" – "Give me a bit of your orange, I gave you a bit of mine."—"Come on, you promised." People say things like that every day, educated people as well as uneducated, and children as well as grown-ups.

Now what interests me about all these remarks is that the man who makes them is not merely saying that the other man's behavior does not happen to please him. He is appealing to some kind of standard of behavior which he expects the other man to know about ... It looks, in fact, very much as if both parties had in mind some kind of Law or Rule of fair play or decent behavior or morality or whatever you like to call it, about which they really agreed. And they have. If they had not, they might, of course, fight like animals, but they could not *quarrel* in the human sense of the word. Quarrelling means trying to show that the other man is in the wrong. And there would be no sense in trying to do that unless you and he had some sort of agreement as to what Right and Wrong are; just as there would be no sense in saying that a footballer had committed a foul unless there was some agreement about the rules of football.

If the reader is not familiar with *Mere Christianity*, I would urge him or her to buy it. The first chapter alone is worth the cost of the book. It is a brilliant piece of psychology. In it, Lewis sums up two crucial aspects of the human condition. We can see the first aspect in the passage quoted. Human beings do quarrel in the way Lewis describes. We are moral agents who cannot help feeling that there are some things we ought to do, and that there are other things we ought not to do. We believe, sometimes despite ourselves, that there is such a thing as right and wrong, and that there are certain principles of conduct to which we and all other human beings ought to adhere. In our dealings with other people we constantly appeal to those principles. We are quick to notice when others violate them. We get defensive and make excuses when it appears that we have violated them ourselves. We get defensive even when no one else is around. We accuse ourselves when no else does, and we rationalize our behavior in front of our consciences just as we would in front of another person. We cannot help applying to ourselves the principles we firmly believe apply to all. To use Alvin Plantinga's term, the belief in morality is basic. Even when we reject that belief in our theoretical reasoning, it comes back to haunt us at every turn. We can never really get away from it. There is a reason why our legal system defines insanity as the inability to tell right from wrong: people who lack that ability have lost an important part of their humanity. They have taken a step down towards the level of beasts.

Even if, in our heart of hearts, we all believe in morality, we do not necessarily share the exact same moral values. Differences regarding values are at least a part of what we quarrel about. Yet Lewis correctly recognizes that our differences in this area never amount to a total difference. The moral beliefs human beings entertain display broad cross-cultural similarities. Ancient Egyptians did not appreciate having their property stolen any more than we do. A brother's murder, a wife's infidelity, or a friend's betrayal would have angered them, just as it angers us. Human nature has not changed much for tens of thousands of years. It does not change at all when one travels to the other side of the globe.

I did not believe Lewis the first time I read him, or even the second time. This idea, that there is a fundamental underlying unity to the moral fabric of humanity, is a hard one to accept. Think about those suicidal fanatics who crashed planes into the World Trade Center. They "knew" they were doing the right thing, that Allah would reward them in heaven with virgins galore. How radically different from our own values the values of some Muslims must seem! Yet there is common ground. Even the most militant Muslims despise thieves, cheats, and liars, just as Christians, Jews, and atheists do. They value loyalty and friendship, just as we do. They love their children and their parents, just as we do. They even condemn murder, at least within their own societies. It is only when they deal with outsiders like us that some of them may seem like (and in fact, be) monsters. To distinguish between insiders and outsiders, and to treat the latter horribly, is actually not so unusual in human history. Expanding one's "inside group" until it encompasses all of humanity is something of an innovation. When we consider all this, the moral gulf between us and them does not seem so unbridgeable.[16] Our admittedly great differences occur against a background of fundamental similarities, similarities guaranteed by the fact that we are all stuck being human. So it seems Lewis was right, despite my earlier skepticism. Universal moral themes can and do underpin the diversity of our moral opinions.

The second point Lewis makes is also right on the money. We cannot escape our moral standards, but we cannot consistently adhere to them either. We have to be moral agents, but we make poor ones. We frequently find ourselves doing what we know is wrong. We can be real scoundrels. Lewis summarizes that first chapter as follows:

These, then, are the two points I wanted to make. First, that human beings, all over the earth, have this curious idea that they ought to behave in a certain way, and cannot really get rid of it. Secondly, that they do not in fact behave in that way. They know the Law of Nature; they break it. These two facts are the foundation of all clear thinking about ourselves and the universe we live in.

Let us examine these central features of the human condition as identified by Master Lewis. The first surely supports the notion that moral statements have truth values. When we make statements of a moral nature we are, of course, expressing our personal feelings. We are also speaking at least partly in the imperative mood, telling others what (we want them) to do. Yet moral statements enjoy a logical status quite different from either pure expressions of feeling, or bare commands. To issue a moral statement is to ground one's feelings and/ or commands in an impersonal, and hence objective, standard. Moral statements justify as well as express feelings. They do not just give commands; they give the reasons for them. Moral statements, then, cannot be mere matters of taste and opinion. They essentially involve an appeal to principles that transcend both the wishes of any one individual, and the customs of any one culture or society. That there are such principles, and that we cannot really escape from them, are points Lewis successfully illuminates. It thus seems very plausible to suppose that when our moral statements appeal to these principles in an appropriate and rational manner, they deserve to be called truths.

There can also be geometric truths. But as we have seen, there are many systems of geometry. Each geometry is internally consistent. Each adheres to all the laws of logic. The various geometries have much in common: there are points, lines, and planes in them all. In every geometry, three-sided figures are called triangles, figures with four equal sides and four equal angles are called squares, and so on. Yet the geometries are mutually incompatible. Their initial assumptions differ, and while these differences may appear slight at first, they lead to dramatically different results.

Could morality resemble geometry in this regard? Could there be different moralities such that each was internally consistent and logically rigorous? Could they all adhere to the common principles of humanity, while still differing to some extent in their assumptions, and could these differences in their starting points lead them to dramatically different and incompatible conclusions?

I believe this to be the case. Human nature is nothing if not plastic. Our genes determine the basic brain structures from which all our thoughts emerge. Those structures must of course obey all the descriptive laws of physics, chemistry, and physiology. They also make it possible for us to follow two prescriptive sets of laws: the laws of logic and what C. S. Lewis referred to as the Law of Nature, meaning a Law of Right and Wrong. But the rationality and humanity built into human nature do not lock us in to any one conception of morality. They do not determine all the details, fix all of our assumptions, set our definitions for us, or preordain every conclusion. It is this flexibility in human nature that makes multiple moralities possible. From among those possibilities, we have the freedom to choose. Our freedom is pretty severely constrained by the prescriptive laws just mentioned, but we are still allowed some wiggle room.

Human beings do differ in their moral views, but this fact alone does not prove the point I wish to make. There could still be just one true morality, and perhaps all the variety in our opinions proves nothing, except our persistent tendency to, in Lewis' words, "get our sums wrong." What does prove my point, I think, is our frequent inability to resolve moral disputes through rational argument. One could attribute this inability to our stubbornness (we refuse to accept even cogent arguments when the conclusion is unpalatable to us), or to our lack of inventiveness (perhaps the argument that would conclusively settle a dispute never occurs to us). However, even though human stubbornness and obtuseness are admittedly pervasive, they do not fully explain the intractability of our moral disagreements. Something else is going on here.

Consider the question, is abortion ever morally permissible? Some would say no, it is never permissible.

Abortion is simply murder. To them this is not a matter of taste or opinion. They do not feel as though they are merely expressing their emotions. It would be more accurate to say that they are giving voice to a very urgent and authoritative moral intuition regarding the sanctity of human life and the importance of protecting all members of our species, even the unborn. Out of respect for this powerful intuition, they might simply define murder as the unnecessary taking of any human life, and they might postulate as an axiom that human rights begin with conception, because even a fertilized egg is still a human being, and there cannot be human beings without human rights. They would see the right to life as being the first right acquired, for without this right, all the others mean nothing. From this constellation of definitions and axioms, it does follow that abortion is murder. So these pro-life advocates have not gotten their sums wrong, they have simply used their moral intuitions to guide their choice of moral definitions and axioms, and then they have drawn the appropriate and rational conclusion. This is exactly how moral thinking should work. No argument could refute their position, because their position is logically sound.

Yet I do not agree with them. My own view is that we possess rights, not in virtue of our being human, but because we are people. One does not have to be human to be a person. If there were Klingons and Vulcans in the world, they too would be people, because they would possess the properties that define people: consciousness, rationality, and a capacity for moral agency. It is just an historical accident that in our world, all the people we will ever meet will belong to our own species. Yet belonging to this species does not automatically confer personhood. A fertilized egg is human. However, since it does not yet enjoy consciousness, rationality, or moral agency, it is not yet a person. It does not yet have rights. It follows that aborting it does not violate anyone's rights, and hence is not murder.

I would venture the hypothesis that the acquisition of rights does not commence until after the mother has had the opportunity, first to discover her pregnancy, and then to decide whether it is best to bring that pregnancy to term. We need not wait any longer than that to begin recognizing in the fetus a child endowed with rights. Rights, we might say, belong not only to current persons such as ourselves, but also to former as well as future persons. Former persons, i.e., the deceased, have rights, which we honor whenever we act in accordance with someone's last will and testament. In the same spirit we might honor the rights of a future person, who for now is still in the womb. The transition from mere embryo to future person occurs as soon as a pregnant woman makes that irrevocable decision to become a mother. The first right any future person must acquire is the right to life, for the reason noted before.

This, then, is the pro-choice perspective. I believe it is just as defensible as the pro-life stance. It does not get its sums wrong. Its conclusion does follow from its definitions and axioms. But since the pro-choice and pro-life advocates start from different definitions of murder, and also from different axioms regarding rights, they naturally arrive at mutually incompatible theorems. We pro-choice advocates cannot be argued out of our position, any more than our pro-life friends can. We too, have our moral intuitions, and we try to give voice to these in our moral reasoning. In this matter, our intuition concerns the primacy of human happiness as the goal of moral endeavors, and the idea that happiness is more likely to be achieved when every newborn child is truly wanted. No doubt our pro-life friends share this intuition, just as we share theirs. But moral intuitions can be vague and conflicting entities. They do not fall into order by themselves. We must hammer them into a moral perspective. There can be more than one way to do this. From identical sets of bricks, people can make very different homes.

28

Our reflections have led us to a kind of moral pluralism. Many thinkers have taken pluralism to imply subjectivism, that is, the view that there is no truth to moral statements at all. The inference from pluralism to subjectivism, however, is unwarranted. There can be truth in morality, even though there are many moralities, just as there can be truth in geometry, despite the existence of multiple geometric systems. A geometric system represents a body of truths because of its logical structure. Its theorems are not thrown together randomly, but instead emerge from a coherent set of definitions and axioms in accordance with the laws of logic. This entitles us to view each theorem as an instance of P^λ. Moral statements can also express P^λ by emerging from a coherent moral framework grounded in rationally intelligible definitions and axioms. These in turn can derive their force and appeal from the way they reflect Lewis' law of nature, as it appears to us, via our moral intuitions.

Moral pluralism may seem very unsatisfying. We would all prefer that our own moral perspective be proven The One True Way. Alas, this is not to be. Our discussion of abortion has shown why. On numerous other issues we could find different conclusions being reached, not because people are making mistakes, but because they are interpreting moral law differently, giving different weights to different intuitions, adopting different definitions of moral terms, and so on. Moral pluralism is just how things are. The pluralism presented here does at least preserve the concept of moral truth. It thus affirms what we all pretheoretically know, namely, that reality has a moral dimension, that there is an "ought" to things, not just an "is."[17]

29

The reality of moral truth has consequences for the theory of possible worlds. We have portrayed **B** as a flat plane, with color-coded sections to indicate the various sets of laws in different worlds. But I did say we could have some fun with this concept, so why not add some texture to the map? Worlds must differ in their moral value, so let that value be represented on the map by elevation. This gives us a map with hills and valleys. There can be great heavenly mountains as well as hellish sinkholes. Uninhabited regions can be marked as desert.

Mathematical truths connect us to reality "in the right way" by helping us to locate W_r in the appropriate "country." Without mathematics we could not discover the scientific laws that define countries. Mathematics adds color to the map. Moral truths also connect us to reality, though in a way different from mathematics. Containment theory captures this notion by saying that morality is what turns our political map of **B** into a relief map. Moral values determine which way is "up." If we view W_r not as an eternally fixed entity, but as having an open-ended future we help create, then moral values fix the gradient we need to climb to make the world a better place.

Better how? Better for whom? Rival moralities will answer these questions differently. But the moral law creates some features for the landscape that are not arbitrary. Worlds with life have more value than those without. Worlds containing rational beings are better than worlds sporting nothing more advanced than bacteria. God, if he existed, would be the rational being *par excellence*. So, by this logic, a world created and governed by God ought to be worth more than a Godless world. There *ought* to be a God. But is there one? Here, once again, Hume's chasm looms large, for "ought" does not imply "is."[18]

Third Essay:
Does God Exist?

1

I accepted C. S. Lewis' insights concerning the law of nature in order to show how moral truth is possible. From the vagueness of the law, its openness to interpretation, I inferred moral pluralism. But Lewis did not introduce the concept of a moral law in order to defend a theory concerning the logical status of moral statements. Instead, he wanted to infer from the existence of the moral law to the existence of God. Lewis thought the law implied a Law Giver.

The moral law, Lewis noted, is prescriptive. It tells us what we ought to do. This distinguishes it from what we ordinarily call the laws of nature, which are descriptive. They describe how natural things actually behave. So those laws may simply be facts about the world. Yet the moral law cannot be a fact about the material world—it does not describe that world. Nor can the moral law be merely our fiction, for we do not control it, and we cannot escape it. The moral law must therefore be a fact about something else. It must point to a reality beyond the universe. Someone must have enacted that law in order to communicate instructions to us.

Now, suppose there were an immensely powerful, loving, and supremely moral God. Wouldn't God care deeply about the moral character of his creatures? Would he not wish to install in them a moral law, to guide them towards the path of righteousness? Of course he would. And what we would expect of such a God is precisely what we find. The world does contain rational beings, namely us, who possess an internal moral compass. Is that not powerful evidence for the existence of God?

This is the argument from morality. Like so many arguments for the existence of God, the argument sounds compelling at first, only to fall apart under examination. We have to pay very careful attention to the argument's logical form to expose its flaws.

The argument from morality appears to have the following logical form: "If P, then Q. Q, therefore P." Putting some meat on these bones, we get this: "If there were a God, then we would expect his rational creatures to be endowed with a moral compass. There are such creatures, and they do have the required endowment. Therefore God exists." Clearly, this is not a valid deductive argument. For example, Socrates, as all logicians know, was mortal. So let Q be the indubitable fact, "Socrates was mortal." Let P be "Socrates was a duck." Certainly, if Socrates was a duck, then Socrates must also have been mortal, because all ducks are mortal. And we know Socrates was mortal. Therefore,

Socrates was a duck, right? Well, no, that does not wash. However, we can easily clean up the argument to make it more rigorous. All we have to do is recast the argument so that it enjoys the same form scientists employ when reasoning inductively about their evidence.

Consider an archeologist who finds ruins, bronze implements, and broken pottery in the middle of nowhere. He knows that these are not naturally occurring items. They only occur where people have been, because only people can make them. The archeologist thus feels entitled to infer that people must once have lived at the site. If the ruins are large, the implements numerous, and pottery debris substantial, then a whole city must have been there.

The archeologist's reasoning displays a logical form along these lines: "If P, then Q, but if not-P, then not-Q. Q, therefore P." Fleshing this out, we get: "If a city had been located there, then we would expect to find the place littered with ruins, bronze tools, and pottery bits. But such things would not be at the site, unless the city had existed. We have found ruins and the like at that location. Therefore, a city must once have been at that location." This is acceptable inductive reasoning.

Put into this same format, the argument from morality looks like this: "If there were a God, then we could expect to find within ourselves a moral law instructing us what to do, and representing his commands to us. Were there no God, no such set of commands would exist. But there is a moral law. Therefore God exists."

To be compelling, an argument must meet two conditions: its logical form must be valid, and its premises have to be true. We have just seen how the argument from morality can be presented in a logically valid form. Unfortunately, one of the premises is false. It is simply not the case that if there were no God, there would be no moral law. This is where the argument from morality fails.

We are subject to two sets of prescriptive laws: the moral law, and the laws of logic. The first set has to do with our actions, the second with our thoughts. As for the laws of logic, it seems clear that God could not have created them. He cannot alter them. They hold for all worlds, even the unfurnished $\mathbf{W}_{\emptyset}$. God would display his wisdom not by crafting the laws of logic wisely, but by wisely putting his thoughts into conformity with them. The same must be true of the moral law. God would exhibit his virtue not by making good moral laws, but by obeying those laws perfectly.

If it seems strange to speak of God obeying anything, just ask yourself if God could have made it laudable to rape women, rob banks, or commit murder? Certainly he could not. Divine decrees permitting rape, robbery, and murder would not change morality. They would only prove that God was an omnipotent monster. We might also add that even in a godless world, rape, theft, and murder would still be abhorrent. God's decrees cannot make them any more so. God's existence or nonexistence has no more affect on morality than it does on logic. God, being omnipotent, could do any logically possible thing, but determining fundamental prescriptive laws is not logically possible, and so does not fall within the domain of God's infinite power. The moral law thus provides no evidence either for or against the existence of God. That law is independent of him, just as logic is.

But the amazing thing is that we are aware of the moral law. Where did that awareness come from, if not from God? Our capacity for moral agency arose through natural Darwinian processes, just as our capacity for rational thought did. We have both of these capacities because they were useful to our ancestors. Granted, doing the right thing does not always increase one's reproductive success, or help us emerge victorious in the struggle for existence. Sometimes behaving morally will even hold us back. Still, moral agency is a powerful thing. An animal that could adhere to moral rules, keep promises, and empathize with others would possess an incredibly valuable set of social skills. Those skills might well have provided benefits that far outweighed their cost. An animal like that would not even be an animal any more, but a person, and the sophistication of his thoughts and actions would give him an edge over less moral rivals. There is thus no reason why natural selection could not have favored those hominids who somehow stumbled upon the trick of behaving morally.

But if our moral sentiments could have arisen naturally, then it would appear superfluous to posit a supernatural cause for them. Our moral awareness did not have to come from God, not in the way that pottery shards and bronze tools have to come from human craftsmen. The "if not P, then not Q" portion of Lewis' argument is thus groundless. When we remove it, the argument collapses.

2

It is fascinating how people can draw opposite conclusions from the same facts. C. S. Lewis examined the human condition and found it to have two central features. From the first, concerning our awareness of a moral law, Lewis inferred the existence of God. He saw the moral law within us as evidence that God loves us and cares deeply about how we conduct our lives. From the second feature, that people are immoral, Lewis concluded that God must be angry with us. We have cause to be uneasy, Lewis said, because we are rebelling against God's commands. By "uneasy" he really meant terrified. What could be more terrifying than having to face the wrath of God?

I accept Lewis' facts, but not his interpretation. God, if he existed, could decree any laws he pleased. He could instill them in our souls, expect us to obey them, and punish us if we did not. But his decrees would not be the moral law, just God's effort to enforce that law. God's decrees, for all their terrifying magnificence, would still be part of the world's furniture. They would belong to the "is" of things. The moral law belongs to the "ought." And between the "is" and the "ought" there is an unbridgeable chasm, as we learned from Hume.

I have a conscience. I can tell right from wrong. I know that there is an "ought" to things, not just an "is," and so there is something like a moral law. But I am not aware of there being any divine commands implanted within me. My ability to tell right from wrong does not seem any more mysterious to me than my ability to walk on my hind legs. Neither ability points to the supernatural.

Let us turn our attention to the second feature Lewis discussed. If we look inside ourselves and examine our souls, we do not like what we see. Our souls can be pretty slimy. We could be better if we tried, but we are not going to try that hard, are we? It is just not in us. Even the greatest effort would only take us so far. Our talent for virtue is very limited.

One has to wonder why God would make slime like us. Couldn't an omnipotent being have done better? If he cared about us as much as Lewis believed, he would have done better. Yet here we are, and we are slime. This ought to cast doubt on God's existence. In fact, when put into the proper perspective, the structure of human nature is proof that no God exists.

"How absurd!" I can hear the reader exclaiming. "Arguments purporting to prove the existence of God may not work, but everyone knows you cannot disprove God's existence either. God is not an empirical hypothesis to be tested against our observations. Nothing we discover about ourselves or the world can ever prove that there is no God."

I beg to differ. There are tests we can perform to determine whether our world was created by God. Our world fails those tests—or is it God who fails them? It does not matter. Either way, it is possible to construct an argument that proves there is no God. I can put the argument in a valid form, using premises known to be true. The argument will thus be logically compelling. The form will be, "If P then Q, but not-Q, therefore not-P," where "P" is the proposition that God exists. One of the key premises will be the very point C. S. Lewis made so well, that human beings do such a pathetic job of obeying the moral law.

It may sound as though I am about to trot out some version of the argument from evil. Such is not the case. Every theist has heard that argument before, made his peace with it, and moved forward with his faith renewed. He comes to believe that the world's suffering is all part of God's inscrutable plan. If we understood the plan, we would thank God even for the evils that plague us, because we would see the good that ultimately comes out of them. We cannot always see the good, of course, since our finite intelligence cannot fathom the infinite mind of God. Thinking along these lines, the theist submits his reason to God's will, and accepts that there is a purpose to everything, even to the worst that life has to offer.

The argument from evil can shake, but not destroy, this faith in God, which makes the argument, ultimately, a failure. However, I want to review the argument from evil in some detail before presenting my own. To understand why my argument works, we need to see why the argument from evil does not.

One has to wonder about this inscrutable plan God is said to have. Why, for example, does God stand idly by while men rape women? Please do not tell me that God will display his justice by punishing the rapists in hell. It is always better to prevent a crime than to punish a criminal. Human societies need systems of justice to punish criminals because they lack the power to prevent the crimes. Unable to prevent, we settle for the second best option, which is to punish. With infinite power at his disposal, though, God would not need to punish. He could simply prevent, displaying his wisdom and foresight by arranging affairs in the world so that rapes did not occur in the first place.

God could have produced a rape-free world in any of several ways. God could zap would-be rapists with tiny lightning bolts. Think of them as jolts from the divine stun gun. The intended victims would get away and, after getting jolted a couple times, would-be rapists would no doubt see the light and start following the path of righteousness. For many of them, God's aversion therapy would not only make them behave better, but lead them to become better people. Virtue, as Aristotle noted, is a matter of developing the right habits. Divinely administered shocks could be God's way of teaching men virtue. With the right habits in place, the jolts of conscience would make the threat of real physical jolts unnecessary.

No one would mind if God intruded into the natural order in this way. Women would appreciate the help. The men ought to be grateful too. A few zaps are surely better than eternal torment. Yet God would not have to be so obvious and heavy-handed. He could instead arrange affairs so that the local constable always just happened to show up in the nick of time to arrest the perpetrator. A police taser could then do the job of the divine stun gun. God might prefer this option. Why should he do things for us, when he can empower us to do them for ourselves? That brings to mind an even better option. Why not empower women to defend themselves without police assistance? Imagine a world in which the threat of being raped gave women super strength. They experience a rush of adrenaline and testosterone so powerful that for a few seconds they can punch like Mike Tyson. Women could then deliver the required jolts themselves, directly to their attackers' faces.

All of these options presuppose the existence of men who wish to rape women. But why would God create such men in the first place? He could have structured male brains so that centers of arousal and aggression did not activate at inappropriate moments. Men's private parts would go limp as soon as a woman said "no." Jolts of any kind would be unnecessary. When it comes to preventing rape, God's infinite power would give him countless options. We need to keep our imaginations open to those options.

Theologians will worry that abolishing rape by any of the methods I have described would eliminate human freedom by depriving us of a real choice between good and evil. We all believe freedom to be a good thing. No one, however, really believes that human beings ought to be free to commit horrible crimes such as rape. We neither covet such freedom for ourselves nor wish others to have it. Why do we lock our doors at night, hire police officers, or take karate lessons, if we want our fellow men to be free to beat, rob, and rape us? The belief that human beings should have a real choice between raping and not raping is one entertained only by theistic apologists, and even then only when they are engaged in apologetics. The rest of the time, they acknowledge that there are some "freedoms" no one should possess.

Imagine living in a world where every would-be rapist really did get zapped by God, arrested by police officers, or punched out by their intended victims. Would you lament the lack of "freedom" in that world? Would you yearn to return to this one? No, you would not. Instead you would praise God for his mercy toward women, and for the superior justice of his creation. "How wise God is!" you would cry. And you would be right. The world just described really would be superior to this one, all things considered. I believe this thought experiment proves the theologians' objection to be poorly grounded.

Groundless or not, the theologians' objection only applies to the scenario in which would-be rapists are physically restrained by some external force. It does not address the other scenarios in which men simply do not desire to rape. So, imagine a world in which men's brains have been rewired so that they never feel tempted to commit rape. Is freedom compromised in such a world? No. Freedom is about power, not desire. A man is free to do whatever he has the power to do. He may have the power to perform many actions he has no desire to perform. Having a real choice between good and evil does not entail being constantly tempted to do horrible things. A man who never wishes to harm women is not any less free because of that. Lack of such desires does not make him a robot programmed for good, just a really nice guy. It follows that God could have designed men's brains so that the urge to brutalize women would not appear. He could have arranged for that without destroying human freedom.

Try another thought experiment. Imagine waking up tomorrow morning and discovering that you have lost one of your vices. The desire for that particular form of sin is gone. Would you feel less free? If anything, you would feel freer. I am sure that is how you would describe this wonderful occurrence. You would say that you were finally free of whatever temptation had been getting the best of you all these years. Now imagine waking up with one more vice, instead of one less. Make it something quite wicked—perhaps the urge to molest children or murder your boss. Would this new desire augment your freedom by producing additional opportunities to make real choices between good and evil? I think not. What increases is not your range of choices, but only the likelihood of your making the wrong choice.

Suppose, though, that God saw some value in temptation. Maybe he thinks the heroic effort it takes to resist temptation is good for our souls. That sounds insane, but even if God did believe that, it would still be possible for him to produce a world without rape. He could structure the human brain so that the centers of reason, foresight, and conscience would be bigger, with a more sophisticated network of neural connections. This would make it almost impossible for the brain's higher order functions to get overridden by the baser impulses. People could then feel temptations, just as they do now, but thanks to their more advanced neural architecture, they would not succumb to them. They could practice heroic temptation resistance all day long without ever committing any sins.

Someone might complain that I want God to program us, as if we were computers. This objection is absurd. Higher-order functions such as reason and conscience are what make us human. It is through them that we become capable of making truly free choices. Designing our brains differently would not mean programming us for virtue. It would mean freeing us from the instinctive programming already embedded in our heads. We would still have those instincts, of course. We need those. But our control over those instincts would be greater. We would be freer than we are now, and, in a sense, more fully human.

If God permits rape, he must be doing it for a reason. This idea sounds plausible at first, even if we cannot imagine what the reason would be. We all know what it is like to suffer through unpleasant means in order to achieve desirable ends, so we sometimes pretend that God acts in the same way. He tolerates an evil, such as rape, in order to achieve his ends, whatever they are. Unfortunately, this analogy between us and God will not survive examination. We have no control over the laws of cause and effect, so if the path to a desirable effect lies through deplorable causes, there is nothing we can do about that. We must either accept those causes, or forgo the effect. God suffers from no such limitation. He does control the laws of cause and effect. If he wishes to achieve some end, he can make that end the effect of whatever causes might be most acceptable to him. It seems wildly implausible, then, that God's ends should ever depend upon means as deplorable as rape.

There is one analogy between us and God that I believe does hold up. God, like us, is a moral agent. He is therefore aware of the moral law, even more so than we are, and is just as obligated to obey it. His infinite power does not confer infinite rights. He is not entitled to do anything he pleases. On the contrary, his infinite power comes with infinite obligations and a fiduciary responsibility to his creation. God's obligations and responsibilities limit his rights, so that, again like us, there are some things God ought to do, and other things he has no right to do.

I do not believe any solution to the problem of evil can surmount the hurdle we have just raised. For if there is anything God has no right to do, it is to create rapists and allow them to brutalize women. Any mere mortal who witnessed a rape being committed would have a moral obligation to help the victim, either by thwarting the rapist himself, or by dialing 911. Doesn't the moral law confer the same obligation on God? God could honor that obligation in any of several ways, without depriving mankind of any important freedom. We have already reviewed some of them.

Theists might point out that suffering often makes us better people. We grow the most and learn the most from our worst experiences. Exposing us to a world riddled with apparently random and pointless evil might be God's way of strengthening us so that we can be better prepared to enjoy the rewards of heaven. This world, they might say, is merely a training camp for the next. We should not complain if the training is hard.

Maybe some people find this kind of talk ennobling. I find it disgusting. A God who thinks that the way to make women better people is to have them beaten and raped is a demented God, unworthy of anyone's worship. Once again I must insist that God would have options. There are other ways to improve someone's character (positive role models come to mind). Besides, the present system, whereby God "trains" us by making us suffer, does not appear to be working. Even with all the suffering there is in the world, we are still pretty slimy, and will remain so, no matter how often God lets us rape, rob, and murder one another. It would be very odd if God were to choose a program of human improvement where the cost in suffering was so great, and where the return on investment, measured by the virtue or wisdom produced, was so pitiful.

Theists may still feel that we have not proven our case. They will cling to the hope that there is a divine plan that lends meaning to all our suffering. While evil may provide a reason to doubt God's existence, it also provides a motive to accept his existence. For the more evil people find in the world, the more powerfully they yearn for God and wish to believe that he is there. To a theist, the pervasiveness of evil does not destroy faith, but merely presents a roadblock along the path to a deeper faith. The roadblock gets pushed aside with repeated assertions to the effect that God works in mysterious ways, his ways are not our ways, and so on.

The argument from evil, my version of it, anyway, does rely on the premise that human beings have rights which even God is not authorized to violate. This premise flows naturally from the conception of moral law outlined earlier. If the moral law is not God's invention, but is in some sense above him, and something he ought to obey, then God is a moral agent just as we are. There must be things even he cannot ethically do, rights even he should not violate. The idea that human beings have rights, and are entitled to a certain dignity, even before God, is one I find ennobling. Many theists, however, will find the idea blasphemous. If God made us, then we are his property, and he may do with us as he pleases. He violates no one's rights no matter what he does, because in his presence we have no rights but those he chooses to give us. The pots have no business complaining about the potter.

Accepting the human-beings-are-chattel theory makes resolving the problem of evil absurdly easy. When good happens, God is being merciful and loving. When evil happens, he is dispensing his justice, teaching us a lesson, testing our faith, or simply exercising his property rights (no doubt for inscrutable reasons).

Accepting the notion that we have God-independent rights makes solving the problem of evil impossibly hard. We could not then justify an evil merely on the grounds that some good came out of it. We would have to ask if anyone's rights were violated, and whether God could have produced the same or comparable goods with less suffering. Our reflections concerning rape show, I think, that such questions cannot be answered in any way compatible with theism. Isn't it obvious that rape violates a woman's rights, that it is not justified by the good that allegedly comes out of it, and that equal or greater goods might have been produced without the use of such horrid means?

Theists are thus obliged to reject my theory of rights. I think they have gotten their sums wrong. They are showing a complete lack of appreciation for the ontological status of the moral law. Turning all men into chattel seems a terrible price to pay for the sake of keeping one's God. I would sooner believe in an omnipotent demon, and then try to solve the resulting problem of good, than believe in God, and "solve" the problem of evil by making myself his property. I am not even sure what difference there is between a demon and a God who thinks of me as one of the slaves on his plantation. But these are personal feelings that theists clearly do not share. If theists are willing to pay the price for their belief in God, the argument from evil will not change their minds. The argument bounces off the armor of their faith.

3

The argument from evil struck at God's goodness. God survived that attack, if only by hiding behind a watered down conception of what it means for him to be "good." Still, he survives, and so the door to faith is not yet shut. To shut it, we need to leave the argument from evil behind and move on to something else. We will need to strike, not at God's goodness, but at his wisdom. This is the Achilles heel of theism. Theists may accept a morally questionable deity, but not a foolish one. To expose the weakness of theism at this point, we must undermine the notion of a divine plan.

I call my argument the argument from artifacts. The strategy is to take the traditional design argument and turn it on its head. Instead of using the design concept to defend belief in God, I will employ it to attack that belief. In adopting this strategy I am actually paying the design argument a compliment. I think that argument contains an important insight. Here, as with the allegory of the cave and the parable of the tea cups, we can refashion something of value and put it to a new purpose.

Here is the insight: anything God makes will be extremely well designed for its purpose and will display a very high level of order. This idea rests on an analogy between products of divine creation and products of human manufacture. Human beings make things. Our creations are often well designed, purposive, and highly ordered. Hence, it is very reasonable to suppose that God's creations would have the same features to an even greater degree.

Items manufactured by humans are called artifacts. Items created by God would also be artifacts. To say that something is an artifact is simply to say that an intelligent being made it. We are all familiar with artifacts. We encounter them every day. We recognize them instantly when we see them. Distinguishing artifacts from other things is easy for us because artifacts have properties that naturally occurring objects do not. Again, artifacts display a high degree of order. There is a nonrandom arrangement of parts. Every part is important to the whole. The structure as a whole has a purpose, an end that the maker wishes to achieve. Well-designed artifacts tend to be very efficient. There are no leftover parts. Nothing is wasted. Wise craftsmen will make their artifacts in a way that minimizes their investment of resources, while maximizing functionality.

The classic example of this is a watch. Watches are highly ordered objects with an exquisite arrangement of parts. The watch's parts and structural properties all (or almost all) contribute to the primary goal, which is to tell time. The watch thus serves the purpose assigned to it, and does so quite efficiently.

An artifact may have more than one purpose. Watches often have design features, such as gold plating or an inscription, which have nothing to do with telling time. They serve other purposes: the gold plating pleases the eye, the inscription designates the watch as a gift from a loved one, and so on. Achieving these secondary purposes introduces an extra cost that detracts from the efficiency with which the primary purpose is accomplished. Still, when we take the whole complex of purposes into consideration, a watch, like any artifact, is amazingly efficient.

Luxury items might seem like an exception to this rule. Cadillacs and Porsches cost far more than other cars and get worse mileage. Relative to the goal of getting a driver from A to B, such cars seem extravagantly wasteful of both gas and money. Obviously, however, luxury cars have purposes that go far beyond the bare-bones necessities. When we consider those other purposes, such as speed, power, comfort, and prestige, the appearance of wastefulness disappears. Cadillacs and Porsches actually do accomplish their purposes efficiently. If they were not in some sense cost-efficient customers would not buy them, nor could the manufacturers afford to make them.

Artifacts of a more abstract nature display the same kind of efficiency we see in material goods. Writers who care nothing for printing costs or publishers' profits will still express their thoughts with the fewest possible words. A novelist will never hide two pages of intelligible narration inside two hundred pages of gibberish. On the contrary, every word will be chosen carefully, with an eye to how it contributes to the narrative. Superfluous words get edited out, and good writers will make extraordinary efforts to ensure that they deliver their message in the pithiest of manners.

Just because something can be used for a purpose does not mean it was designed for that purpose. A softball-sized rock, worn smooth by the currents of a stream, might make a pretty good hammer. In a pinch, when no real hammers are available, you might use it to hammer in a nail. But a smooth rock is still a long way from being a hammer. It has no handle. There are no finger grooves to improve one's grip. Being still a mere jumble of different minerals, it will probably break much more easily than the iron head of a real hammer. Extra touches, like a nail pull, are absent. So despite the rock's utility as a hammer, we can still tell, from the details of its composition and structure, that it is not the genuine article.

It seems, then, that naturally occurring items can be accidentally suited to some human purpose. My favorite example of this concept is a cave. People can live in caves. Some of our distant ancestors did live in them. Yet caves are not designed to be dwellings. They are not really designed at all. Caves just exist. It is easy to tell a house from a cave. Houses display an economy of structure that caves lack. If we stumbled upon a cave and mistook it for a house we would certainly be disappointed. "Just look at this awful house!" we would say. "The builder used up tons of rock to make it, yet it is damp and drafty. There are no windows. It doesn't even have indoor plumbing!" When treated as artifacts, caves seem poorly designed.

Most people today live in houses, not caves. We also live in a material universe, so it seems fair to ask whether our universe resembles a house, or whether it is more like a cave. Is the universe designed to be a dwelling for its inhabitants, the way a house is, or is it something we just stumbled into and opportunistically adapted for our own use, the way our ancestors opportunistically exploited caves?

The question just asked is relevant to the question of God's existence. If there is a God, then the universe would be his creation. It would be, in other words, an artifact. What purpose would this artifact serve? Artifacts typically serve some need, but God does not really need anything, does he? He is already perfect. He is supremely provisioned with intelligence, wisdom, power, and every other good his spiritual nature might require. Many artifacts assist in the performance of some task that could not be done otherwise, or at least, could not be done as well. Automobiles can get us to work much faster than if we walked. A hammer pounds nails much better than does a fist. God, however, can perform any task with a mere thought. He thus has no need for material aids.

One might speculate that the universe is God's artwork. It is to him what a painting or sculpture is to a human artist. There is definitely something to that idea, but it cannot be the whole answer. The conceptual powers of human minds are finite. A merely imagined painting is not as vivid as one on canvas, nor the merely imagined sculpture as breathtaking as one carved out of real marble. That is why human artists need canvases and blocks of marble. But the conceptual powers of God would suffer from no such limitation. His thoughts would be as vivid, as detailed, and as real, as anything could be. The divine thoughts would not need embodiment in art because they would be art. The power of God's mind thus put him beyond art. So again we must ask why God would make a universe.

I think there is just one plausible answer to this question: God would need a universe in order to house living creatures. Life is good. It is the one thing that is good not merely for some ulterior purpose, but for its own sake. So God would not rest content with imagining life, even though he could do that with perfect clarity. He would want to make real life, especially intelligent life. Creating intelligent life would represent an opportunity to share with his creatures those special attributes of consciousness and rationality that constitute the divine nature.

This answer not only seems reasonable in itself, it is, I believe, the answer most theists would give. So I am not burdening theists with an unwanted assumption. I am instead accepting an idea already embedded in traditional western monotheism. Indeed, the idea emerges very naturally from the account of creation in the book of Genesis, a book considered sacred by all three of the great religions in the west: Judaism, Christianity, and Islam.[19] In Genesis, humankind is the crowning glory of the six days of creation, and the whole creative process seems aimed at preparing for our appearance.

What does this mean for my argument? If God exists, then the universe is his artifact, and it should display great economy in the attainment of its purpose, which is the creation of (intelligent) life. Every part and aspect of the universe should be designed with that purpose in view. A universe created by God would exist for the sake of his living creatures. It would be their dwelling, and provide the scene for the drama of their lives. It would, in short, be rather like a house. So a house-like universe would be strong evidence for the existence of God. A Godless universe, on the other hand, would be a naturally occurring object, like a cave, something that living creatures could opportunistically make use of, even though it wasn't designed specifically for them. An inefficient, ramshackle, cave-like universe would make a very unlikely and implausible artifact, since it would lack the attributes characteristic of artifacts. Such a universe would create a strong presumption against God's existence.

Now consider how inefficient the universe is compared to a house. Every room in a house is habitable. Most of the universe is uninhabitable. Only an infinitesimal percentage of the universe's substance has any connection to living things. 95% of it is squandered on dark matter and dark energy. The ordinary matter that comprises the remaining 5% could form life sustaining stars and planets, yet most of it does not. Some is simply swallowed up in black holes. About half of all solar systems are binary, meaning that they include two stars swirling around each other. These almost certainly support no life, because the planetary orbits in such systems would be too irregular. Many other stars have, in effect, already died, becoming white dwarfs, red giants, or what have you. Among living stars, it seems probable that most either have no planets, or none that meet the very specific conditions necessary for generating life. Even in our own solar system, the only one known to be inhabited, there is just the one planet that supports living creatures. All the other planets in our system are lifeless masses of rock and gas. This does not mean that we are necessarily alone in the universe. There could be other civilizations out there, perhaps thousands. However, even if there are, those thousands are mere specks in an unimaginably vast and desolate wasteland. Relative to its immense size, then, the universe must be very sparsely inhabited, and the lack of cosmic economy is quite glaring.

God, if he were indeed the infinitely wise architect of the cosmos, could have made our universe millions of times more efficient. Every planet could be teeming with life. Every solar system could be swarming with planets. There does not have to be any wasted energy or unused matter if God is in charge. Do not say that I am suggesting the impossible. This is God we are talking about. For him, all logically possible things are within his power. He could fix the world's initial conditions, amend its laws, or do whatever it took to ensure that the universe produced life, and especially intelligent life, in far greater abundance than it does now. And if he could, then he would, for there would be every reason to do so, and no good reason not to.

When we think about the universe's inefficiency, it seems obvious that the universe is nothing like a house. It lacks the characteristics that would identify it as an artifact. But if it lacks the properties characteristic of an artifact, then it is not an artifact. It is instead a naturally occurring object. The universe is our cave.

"What about the laws of physics?" the reader might ask. "Are those not proof that the universe is highly ordered?" I have to admit that the universe displays an impressive degree of order, and certainly this order derives from its laws. However, if we want to know whether a given object is an artifact, it is not enough to establish that it is ordered. We have to ask whether it displays the kind of order that allows it to achieve efficiently some purpose its maker could be presumed to have. The universe does not display that kind of order, for while the universe may be doing many things, it is not efficiently doing anything.

"But don't the laws of physics seem exquisitely fine-tuned to make life possible, and is it not immensely improbable that the laws should be that way, unless they represent the edicts of a wise creator?" The laws of physics do make life possible. However, this does not prove that they were chosen for that purpose. It simply means that thanks to those laws, our universe meets the bare minimum requirements for habitability. Meeting such minimal requirements does not suffice to make the universe an artifact. No architect, in designing a house, seeks merely to meet the bare minimum requirements of habitability. Even a cave might meet those. Any good architect will aim higher. He will provide his house with design features no cave would have. Mere habitability thus cannot distinguish universes that are like caves from those which are designed to be houses. We need to raise the bar. When we do, and we look for the kind of order typical of artifacts, the universe fails the test. The universe seems much more cave-like than house-like.

As for the alleged improbability of our physical laws, I am not sure what that means. Our world, $\mathbf{W_r}$, is just one of an infinite number of possible worlds. $\mathbf{W_r}$ resides in a "country" on the plane of being that is just one of an infinite number of such countries. So while it might seem immensely improbable that we should get this world, in this country, and not some other someplace else, this sense of improbability is an illusion.

Consider what happens when we throw a pair of dice. There is a state of affairs before the throw, a state after, and a mechanical process that leads from one to the other. If we examine the dice, and understand the mechanics of the throw, we can calculate the probability of any particular outcome. We can also discover the probabilities through brute force, by throwing the dice some very large number of times. Nothing comparable to this can occur when we try to estimate the probability of our physical laws. If our physical laws cover all events throughout all of time, then there was never any state of affairs prior to the laws' operation. Nor was there any process, mechanical or otherwise, that led to their emergence. The brute force method will not work either, since we have just the one universe to contemplate. We cannot venture out onto the plane of being in order to calculate the ratio of habitable versus uninhabitable worlds. Both sets of worlds would have infinite memberships, so in what sense would there be a ratio?

The feeling of improbability comes, I think, from imagining that there was some random process for generating our current set of laws. One might pretend that there was a random number generator picking values for all the physical constants. Perhaps a monkey selected our world to be $\mathbf{W}_r$ by throwing a dart onto the plane of being. Whatever point the tip of the dart landed on became $\mathbf{W}_r$. Given some such process, the probability of arriving at our world, with these laws, might well be zero. The intellectual vertigo this engenders might tempt us to replace the monkey with something smarter. But there was never any process, random or otherwise, for selecting our world or its laws. There was never any time when the world was not. Our world just is; all other worlds just aren't. We might still feel as though we caught a lucky break when our world became $\mathbf{W}_r$ and then somehow stumbled onto just this set of laws, but that feeling is, as I said, an illusion based on an illicit metaphysical fancy.

When we get to the universe and its laws, the concept of probability loses its application. The laws of physics are neither probable nor improbable. They are instead the backdrop against which all probabilities and improbabilities take place.

The claim here is that there is no such thing as *a priori* probability. Readers dubious of this claim may suspect that I have made it in a desperate effort to shore up my atheistic thesis. However, I believe this claim can be proven independently of my larger argument. Just imagine if someone were to ask you which number is more probable, two or seven? The question means nothing unless we specify a number choosing mechanism. If we choose a number by selecting a card from a standard deck, then twos and sevens are equally probable. There is a four-in-fifty-two chance of drawing either. However, if we roll a pair of dice, then the probability of getting a two is only one in thirty-six. An outcome of seven would be six times more probable than that. This proves that probabilities presuppose mechanisms of choice. But when we try to think *a priori*, we have no mechanisms available to us.

My denial of *a priori* probabilities applies, of course, only to empirical propositions. It has no bearing on logically necessary truths, such as those we find in mathematics, which may be said to have an *a priori* probability of one.

Have we dismissed the "fine tuning" argument for the existence of God too quickly? The argument points to an effect, namely the emergence of intelligent life on Earth. It then traces that effect back to a cause, consisting of the whole universe as it existed at the time of the Big Bang. The argument then notes that had the cause been even slightly different, the effect would never have happened. For example, had the total mass of the universe been larger, or had the force of gravity been stronger, the universe might have collapsed in on itself before it could produce living creatures. Other forces too, such as the strong and weak forces, had to be set at very close to their current strength levels. Even rather small changes in certain physical constants would have made life of any kind impossible. So, the argument holds, all these forces, quantities, and physical constants had to be "fine tuned" in advance, for our benefit. It is just as if the universe knew we were coming. And how would the universe know that, unless God orchestrated the show?

The argument seems plausible only because it flatters our ego. When the effect is something as wonderful as ourselves, and the cause is something as magnificent as the universe, we want very much to believe that cause and effect were linked on purpose. But what happens when the cause is less magnificent, and the effect is something deplorable? Let the effect be Hitler's rise to power in Germany in 1933, and let the cause be the state of affairs in Europe circa 1870. We can do the same type of analysis here as we did before. We can honestly say that had the cause been even slightly different, the effect would never have occurred. Could we go back in time and alter any of a thousand variables, then maybe Hitler would never even have been born. His parents might never have met. Perhaps Hitler would have been killed in battle during World War I. Or perhaps his life would simply have taken a different course, and he would have become a successful artist or journalist. It seems wildly improbable that all the historical variables should have been exactly the way they were, and not some other way. But does this mean that some diabolical Nazi god artfully arranged matters to ensure Adolf Hitler's political ascendency? No. That is absurd. This kind of reasoning is clearly fallacious. But let the conclusion be pleasing, and let distinguished scientists dress it up in the language of modern physics, and people fall prey to it.

"You lean heavily on the universe's inefficiency," the reader might continue. "But efficiency is only necessary to finite creatures like us. To God, who is infinite, efficiency is not important." An omnipotent God could certainly afford to be inefficient. Yet those who make this objection are forgetting that God is not only infinitely powerful, but also, by definition, infinitely wise. So, a universe designed by God cannot be just a massively impressive display of power. It must also be an equally impressive display of the divine intelligence. And how does intelligence get displayed in the making of an artifact? In the economy of its arrangements and in the way every part gets put to good use. Efficiency in the achievement of purpose is the sign of intelligent design, and the mark of a master designer.

Human artists take great pains to make their productions the best that they can. Often they take such pains not because they have to, but because they want to, out of love for their work. Would not God do likewise? This is another place where I think we can have confidence in the analogy between human and divine endeavors. If life is good, then more life would be better, and a universe rich in life would be superior to one less densely populated. God could thus be expected to deploy the divine intelligence to craft, not just any habitable universe, but an immensely fecund one. His love for his creation would motivate him to do so. The artifact of an infinitely wise and loving God would be more efficient than any human artifact, not less so. It seems insulting to God to suggest otherwise.

Making the universe an efficient life-producing factory would not have compromised its beauty as an artistic creation. If anything, a universe rich in life would be vastly more beautiful, because of the greater craftsmanship it exhibited. And while the universe is indeed very beautiful just the way it is, it nonetheless lacks the efficiency and purposefulness of arrangements that would mark it as an artifact. The conclusion, then, must be that it is not one.

Arguing to the nonexistence of God from the inefficiency, wastefulness, and apparent pointlessness of the universe is not original to me. The attempt has been made before, with little impact.[20] I believe the logical force of the argument has simply gone unrecognized. Perhaps the logical steps of the argument have not previously been laid out with sufficient clarity. The real problem, however, may lie in a failure of the imagination. Here, as when we discussed the problem of evil, we need to open our imaginations to the options God would enjoy. God did not have to blast huge quantities of matter and energy across the vastness of space, and then hope that, billions of years later, on a few tiny specks of rock, intelligent life would eventually emerge. He could have gotten better results much more quickly. Yet our universe appears to have arrived at intelligent life by the longest, most tedious, and least efficient possible route. How much wisdom can it take to do things that way? It is as if the universe just blundered into us. A universe crafted with life in mind would presumably look quite different. Indeed, compared to what God could have done, the results we have in front of us seem paltry.

From the universe we turn to the living organisms that allegedly constitute its *raison d'être*. Every creature on Earth displays that wonderful economy and purposive arrangement of parts we typically associate with artifacts. This cannot result from chance. Organisms seem designed. In fact, they really are designed, and very well, for the tasks they perform. Fish are marvelously well designed for swimming, birds for flying, tigers for hunting, and so on, throughout the entire animal kingdom. Nor are the other kingdoms any different in this regard. Yet thanks to Charles Darwin, we know that an unintelligent process did the design work. Darwin proved that life evolved. From simple beginnings eons ago, living creatures branched out into a great tree of life. Despite the tremendous diversity we see among them today, all species on Earth are cousins, related by descent from common ancestors. This kinship explains the fundamental underlying unity of life, displayed, for example, in the fact that we find the same genetic code used in literally every living cell on the planet. Darwin also showed that this branching process could occur through natural mechanisms, principally that of natural selection. So if Darwin was right, and the evidence overwhelmingly supports him, then organisms are not artifacts, at least not directly. They are naturally occurring items.[21]

Yet organisms could still be, indirectly, the products of a divine creator. Perhaps God used evolution as the means for achieving his end. Many theists believe that to be the case. Many evolutionary biologists, whether theists or not, insist that there is no contradiction between their science and religious faith. In a Darwinian world, the mere existence of complex living organisms does not prove that God exists. Life could have evolved without the backing of divine intentions. It is not clear, though, that evolution provides any evidence against the existence of God. Why shouldn't a theist see the providence of God at work behind the mechanisms of evolution?[22]

General Motors manufactures Cadillacs in a factory equipped with all kinds of machines. It is making artifacts with the aid of other artifacts. Some of the jobs done with machinery could be done by skilled labor, but the machinery can often do those jobs better, faster, and cheaper. And that is why the machinery is used. The machinery is a good investment. It pays for itself through higher productivity.

If God is using evolution to generate life, then he is doing exactly what General Motors does. He is using artifacts to make artifacts. Living organisms are his artifacts, albeit indirectly, and the mechanisms of evolution are the machinery God employs in his life producing factory. But God did not have to use the evolutionary process. He could have invented some other process, or he could have bypassed mechanisms and created life via acts of the divine will, as in Genesis. So if God chose Darwinian mechanisms as his preferred method, there would have to be a reason for it. As with the machinery in a car factory, Darwinian evolution would have to justify itself by doing the job at hand better, faster, or more efficiently than the alternatives.

The trouble is that Darwinian evolution is probably the slowest and sloppiest mechanism imaginable. Much of the evidence for evolution, in fact, comes from evolution's innumerable engineering gaffes. Evolution has no foresight. It creates adaptive solutions suitable for the moment, then modifies them opportunistically with repeated jerry-rigging. Consider just this one example. The mammalian larynx is connected to the brain by a nerve. This laryngeal nerve once connected the brain to the gills of our distant fish ancestors. When the gills disappeared, the nerve was redeployed for its current use. But that redeployment left it awkwardly placed. When the ancestors of mammals grew necks, something unknown among fish, the laryngeal nerve got displaced even further. The laryngeal nerve in modern mammals thus ends up taking a detour on its route from brain to larynx. The detour may be only a few inches in some animals, but in giraffes, with their long necks, its amounts to several feet. Obviously giraffes can live with this. But is still an absurd engineering gaffe, created by the fact that evolution simply had no idea that fish-like ancestors would ever have giraffe-like descendants. An intelligent engineer, designing a giraffe from scratch, could easily do a better job. But since it lacks intelligence, evolution cannot do so well, and so it produces oddities of the sort described over and over again.[23]

The giraffe's laryngeal nerve seems odd because it achieves a sensible goal in an awkward manner. However, in countless other situations we catch evolution achieving deplorable goals with ruthless efficiency. Viruses, as far as I know, have no redeeming features. Their sole function in the world is to kill living cells and make multi-cellular creatures sick. And they are very good at it. An intelligent engineer who wanted to make animals sick could hardly build a better pathogenic artifact than a virus. Yet for all their engineering perfection, viruses do not make plausible artifacts, simply because the goal at which they seem to aim is one no sane being would wish to see achieved. Nor are viruses alone in being irredeemably harmful. The natural world is full of parasitic creatures who earn their keep by making other creatures suffer.

No human would use a tool for a job if bare hands worked better. If we could pound nails quickly and painlessly with our fists, we would not bother making hammers. But if God is using evolution to produce life, then he is choosing to do with a tool a job he could have done better without tools. That God would waste four billion years allowing evolution to churn out jerry-rigged creatures, when he could easily have created masterpieces of engineering perfection in the biblical six days, seems utterly incomprehensible. That he would torment his jerry-rigged productions with viruses and other micro-monsters seems positively diabolical.

But suppose God wanted nature to produce life without his constant intervention. Perhaps a more autonomous nature would have some appeal to him. Even then God did not have to rely on the Darwinian mechanisms of mutation and natural selection. He could have designed nature in such a way that it would replicate in its organic creations the engineering perfection God would have achieved, had he chosen to do the job of producing life himself. A nature designed in that manner would itself be an example of engineering perfection, and would be a beautiful thing indeed. So it still seems wildly improbable that God would choose Darwinian methods for generating organic forms.

Despite the impressive order living organisms display, the details of their structure demonstrate that no intelligence went into their design. This means they cannot be artifacts, either directly or indirectly. Evolutionary theory does constitute a serious threat to theistic belief.

We must now ask whether we humans might be artifacts. Are we the product of intelligent design? Granted, we evolved in the same way other organisms did. The evidence of evolution is written all over our bodies, just as it is upon the bodies of everything from bacteria to giraffes. But maybe God did not let the mechanisms of Darwinian evolution just mindlessly spit us out. Maybe he took some special care with us. Maybe we really are made in his image.

Suppose, for the sake of argument, that this was in fact the case. What would the evidence for it be? What signs would we find of our divine origins? If we were God's artifacts, then we would be extremely well designed for whatever purpose God assigned to us. We would be as good at achieving that purpose as fish are at swimming, birds are at flying, and tigers are at hunting. But what would our purpose be, if we were God's creatures?

What makes us unique in the animal kingdom is that we have minds. We are both rational and moral agents. I am sure a good God would want what was good for us. Like any loving parent, he would want what was best for his children. But the good of our rational nature is wisdom. Unfortunately, as the first essay made clear, we are not well designed for pursuing wisdom. Human beings make poor philosophers. We can pursue wisdom, thanks to the collection of faculties we inherit as part of our human nature, but many aspects of that nature make the pursuit difficult. Any normal human will find the path to wisdom obstructed by obstacles of which he is only dimly aware, obstacles produced by his faults, foibles, prejudices, and blind spots. So we are never as good at philosophy as tigers are at hunting. We are only as good at it as ducks are at long-distance running. God was not generous when it came to doling out brains to philosophers.

So put wisdom to one side. Perhaps the idea that God cares how wise we are is just a philosopher's conceit. Let us focus on something less tied to the parochial interests of my guild. The great religions of the western world all insist that God cares deeply about our moral rectitude. What were the Ten Commandments about, if God cares not how we act? Why did Christ die on the cross for our sins, if God has no concern for our moral well-being? It seems that if there is a God, and if he is anything like the being theists imagine him to be, then he wants more than anything for us to be good people. He wants us to obey the moral law by living virtuous lives. Doing this would have to be a giant part of our purpose.

Once again we have a problem. We humans are even worse at pursuing virtue than we are at attaining wisdom. I will concede, because I believe it to be true, that in any given situation we are perfectly free to do the right thing. If we do wrong, that too is a free choice. The evil we do is our own fault, and we have no one to blame but ourselves. But our choices do not emerge from a vacuum. They emerge from that crazy hodge-podge of characteristics we call human nature. When it comes to living a moral life, our human nature gets in the way. There is nothing we can do about this. We do not choose our nature.

Think about how bizarre it is that we should be moral agents so little inclined to virtue. But if we look at ourselves through the spectacles of evolutionary biology, it makes a certain amount of sense. Suppose that you could step back in time about a hundred thousand years, to the very origins of modern humans, and design our species yourself. For the sake of argument, imagine that your only goal is to produce humans who make excellent Darwinian survivalists. All you want is for your custom-tuned humans to be really, really good at getting their genes into future generations. How would you proceed?

Your custom-tuned humans will have to be intelligent. They need enough brain power to make sophisticated stone tools and use clever hunting strategies. They need to outwit rivals within their own hunter-gatherer band, and outside it. You should also grant your humans the power of speech. Linguistic skills allow for complex social groups, which are crucial to the recruitment of allies in the struggle for life. But you do not want them too smart. Excess intelligence might make them bored with their hunter-gatherer lives and cause them to do philosophy or astronomy when they should be hunting, fornicating, or making war. So it is not Einsteins you are looking for, but men like Odysseus: clever rather than wise, full of stratagems and practical wisdom, but not too concerned with abstractions.

You could even endow your humans with a conscience. This provides them with an advanced capacity for social skills. But if having a conscience is good, it does not follow that having a strong conscience would be better. You actually want the conscience to be weak. You are not out to produce saints. Saintly behavior may be good for the soul, but it is not good for the propagation of one's genes. So, Saint Francis is not the right model. What you are looking for is a race of men more like Genghis Khan, the conqueror who once defined happiness as the crushing of one's enemy, followed by the possession of his wives and daughters. There only has to be enough conscience to hold the tribe together and maintain honor among the thieves. What you do, then, is endow your humans with a whole bunch of brain structures that can operate independently of conscience and even override it in their pursuit of wealth, power, and women.

It would appear the natural selection actually did more or less as I have suggested. It made us good Darwinian survivalists by endowing us with moderate intelligence, weak consciences, and a strong Schopenhauerian will directed at worldly success. Instead of putting our rational and moral faculties in charge, it created a balance of power, a system of checks and balances, which left reason and conscience to compete with a host of other interests. This leaves us feeling pretty messed up, but so what? Evolution is not about feeling good. It is certainly not about being good. It is only about results.

Human nature makes sense, sort of, when viewed from what Richard Dawkins called the gene's eye point of view.[24] Does it make sense from a God's eye point of view? No. God would be appalled at the kind of people we have become. We are by no means the creatures he would want us to be. Our nature points us toward courses of action he would abhor. In saying this I am doing no more than repeating what C. S. Lewis said at the beginning of *Mere Christianity*. Lewis, in turn, was simply articulating one of the basics of the traditional Christian world view, which has always insisted that we are chronic sinners. But Lewis' conclusion, that God must be angry with us, does not follow. The correct inference is that there is no God. God could not have designed us to be the way we are. Under no circumstances would he have delegated responsibility for designing us to natural selection. He would have foreseen that evolution would botch the job, which, in a way, it did.

That is argument from artifacts, presented from three angles: the human, the organic, and the cosmic. It has, as I noted earlier, the logical structure, "If P then Q, but not Q, therefore not P." If God created us and all living things, together with the material universe, then all of these things would display the characteristics of supremely well-designed artifacts. But they do not display such characteristics. Therefore, God could not have created them. He would be their creator if he existed, so we must conclude that he does not exist.

The argument I have presented seems perfectly decisive. Its chief merit is that it prevents the theist from exploiting the same escape hatch used to evade the argument from evil. Evading the argument from evil was actually easy. All the theist had to do was announce that God allows evil for some unknown purpose, and that it is not for us to figure out what it is, because, well, God works in mysterious ways. That option is not available here. For when we say that the universe and its inhabitants are poorly designed, we have already taken their purposes into account. To say that something is poorly designed means that it is designed poorly relative to the purpose it was intended to serve. It thus makes no sense to suggest that God designed things poorly for a purpose. Poor design is just poor design.

4

I can hear the reader gushing forth with objections, crying, "Your argument assumes what it needs to prove."

"How so?" I might say.

"When defining the term "artifact," you took it for granted that only products of human action are artifacts, and you tailored your definition to fit just those. So naturally, when you examined other things, such as the universe, organisms, and human nature, you concluded that they did not fit your definition. But that is only because you arranged things to guarantee that conclusion."

I see the point the reader is trying to make, but it does not invalidate my argument. The key logical issue here is whether we can identify the distinguishing characteristics of artifacts without prejudging the issues at hand. I think we can. Artifacts are by definition the creations of rational beings. We are rational beings, more or less, so we have inside information concerning what makes a good artifact. We interact every day with objects that we know for certain to be artifacts because humans made them. Thinking about these objects, e.g., watches, houses, automobiles, hammers, and the like, allowed us to identify the traits that make them what they are. A list of distinguishing characteristics could thus be created without any reference to objects whose status is less certain.

With such a list in hand, we turned our attention to things not made by humans. The results of our inquiry were not fixed *a priori*. Nothing prevented the universe from fitting the artifact profile. But the plain fact of the matter is that it did not. The universe lacked the purposive economy of arrangements we associate with artifacts, so we had to conclude that it was not the product of an intelligent creator. Living organisms do display a remarkable ordering in their arrangements. The analogy between them and human artifacts is actually quite close. But even here we find some key elements missing. Organisms frequently have structural flaws that betray a lack of intelligence in their design, and even when well designed, the purpose their design serves is very often not a purpose one could plausibly attribute to an intelligent being. The analogy between organisms and artifacts is thus only that—an analogy, rather than an identity. Organisms are not artifacts, not even indirectly.

We get the same result when we consider human beings. There is no *a priori* reason why human nature could not be a divinely engineered artifact. Yet it too fails the test for artifact status. Human nature got cobbled together through eons of evolution, via the same blind Darwinian mechanisms we find at work everywhere else in nature. We are not well designed for the purpose God would presumably wish us to serve. The baggage of our evolutionary history is a major impediment to doing his will. That would be an absurd result if there really were a God.

"All you are saying is that doing God's will is hard. Well, so what?" the reader might exclaim. "No one said that pursuing virtue was supposed to be easy. God does not owe it to us to make it easy. He gave us the tools we need—reason and conscience—and he gave us the freedom to choose how we use them. I do not know what more he was supposed to do for us. So why are you complaining?"

We have the tools. We have the freedom. What we lack is the talent. Imagine that you run a training facility for the U. S. Olympic swim team. For swimmers, the Olympics are the *summum bonum*. The competition to get there is fierce, so the training you put your athletes through will be grueling. Complaining about this necessary evil would be pointless. But not just anyone will be at your facility. The athletes you pick for your program will be the most talented athletes you can find. You will look for athletes with long arms, strong shoulders, large hands, big feet, and robust cardiovascular systems. These traits will give your swimmers a mechanical advantage in the water, and allow them to endure the endless miles of practice your program demands. The training you offer builds upon that foundation of natural talent. The talent will be wasted without training, but without talent, training is not enough. So your athletes will need lots of both.

Now suppose God did create this world as a training ground intended to prepare souls for the next. Maybe the training here would have to be pretty arduous. We would have no business complaining about that. Getting to heaven would be our *summum bonum*, so we might have to accept suffering as the price of admission. But God would not pick just anyone to put through his training program. From the infinite throngs of logically possible people that dwell in the plane of being, he could choose an elite group to bring into reality. He could custom design his chosen elite for the task at hand. He could endow them with the highest possible natural aptitude for wisdom and virtue. That gift of raw talent would provide the foundation for the training. Talent and training would both be necessary.

My complaint, if you want to call it that, is not that the training is difficult, but rather that we humans do not appear to have the right stuff for it. We are not exactly gifted with abundant talent when comes to being saints and sages. While we may enjoy some of the required qualifications, the total package is just not there. Imagine what it would be like to have a physique designed for race walking, and to be suddenly thrust into an elite swim program. Your wonderful cardiovascular system would help a lot, but you would never become a champion swimmer—your spindly arms, narrow shoulders, and tiny hands would slow you down. In the same way, human beings are endowed with reason and conscience, which helps a lot in terms of allowing us to become the people we should like to be. But many features of human nature slow us down and even propel us onto paths incompatible with wisdom and virtue.

It seems, then, that we are not really designed for the life God would want us to lead. We are designed, not by God for wisdom or virtue, but by natural selection to be Darwinian survivalists. Even by that standard our design is imperfect. Sometimes, from the standpoint of our genes, we are actually too moral and too intellectual. We have been known to do the right thing, even when it does our genes no good. We sometimes pursue things of the mind far beyond any biological need. On the other hand, our baser impulses are sometimes so great, they cause us grave harm. Excesses on both the moral and immoral side are, I suppose, the price evolution pays for making us such clever scoundrels. But we are still closer to being what natural selection would want us to be than we are to what God would want us to be.

I cannot help thinking that such a disastrous state of affairs would be impossible, if God existed. God's divine plan would have to include creating a universe that is well designed for its primary purpose, which is to create life. It would also have to include the creation of rational creatures who are well designed for their primary purpose, which is to pursue wisdom and virtue. Yet these things do not exhibit excellent design relative to those purposes. I believe this undermines the whole concept of a divine plan, so I have to conclude that there is no such plan, and hence, no deity.

"Your argument founders on God's freedom," I can hear the reader replying. "God is perfectly free to make any world he pleases. It follows that every world would be consistent with his existence. This means that no world can be used to prove God doesn't exist."

I agree that if God existed, he could make any universe, and any set of creatures, he pleased. But he would not make just any universe, or just any set of creatures. He would not select things to make at random. Like any skilled craftsman, he would make what best served his ends. Can the reader honestly say that we are the right choice for God to make? Once again, I must urge the reader to consider God's options.

This distinction between what someone can do and what they would do is critical to my argument. What people can do is what they have the power to do, what falls within their range of options. What they would do is usually some small subset of what they can do. What people would do is what it would be in character for them to do. There are thousands of things I could do, but would not even consider doing. I could rob a bank or join a monastery in Tibet, but I won't. Doing those things would not fit my character. I am not tempted to go in those directions. The reader too, I am sure, has many things within his power to do that he absolutely, positively will not do, because he or she thinks that doing them would be immoral, foolish, or absurd.

My argument, then, in a nutshell, is that God could easily have made us so that we would be both free and good. We would be perfectly free to choose either good or evil, but we would also be good, simply because we would rarely if ever be tempted to choose the latter. Evil, in other words, would fall within the large circle of things we could do, but not within the smaller circle of things we would do. Freedom from temptation would not turn us into virtuous robots. We would still be people, only better, and freer too. Our susceptibility to sin is not what makes us free. If anything, it renders us less free by enslaving us to our passions.

Nothing would prevent God from designing us in the way I have described. God, if he existed, would himself be both perfectly free and perfectly good, and so creatures made in his image could also have that character, finite and embodied though they might be. But if God could make us in that fashion, then he would. To saddle us with all our present foibles and liabilities unnecessarily would be crazy.

"Yet God, for whatever reason, did make us, foibles and all. Is it not better to have made us, than not to have made us?" the reader might ask. This question inappropriately narrows God's options down to just two: either he makes us and puts us here in this universe, or he makes nothing. A better question would be, what could God have made in our place? What other rational species might occupy the Earth? Is it plausible to suppose that after reviewing all the possibilities, God would decide that we were the elite corps of spiritual champions he wanted to train for the joys of heaven? Us? Really?

Theists will tell me that I am being arrogant. God's wisdom, they will say, is infinitely beyond my understanding. Who am I to tell him what to do? Alas, this strategy backfires, for the more I contemplate God's infinite nature, the more convinced I become that he would not have made a fool as wretched as I. A God so great would have created a greater universe and populated it with greater people. Any creation of his would have been, not merely greater than what we have in front of us, but even greater than what our limited powers can imagine.

So I am not trying to tell God how to run things. All I am saying is that postulating God as the cause of our universe is rather like postulating an atom bomb to explain a pothole. The more powerful we imagine the bomb to be, the more puzzling that tiny pothole becomes. Given the immensity of the bomb, should the crater it produces not be larger? So with God: the more exalted we imagine his attributes to be, the less plausible it becomes to suppose that he would make us, or our world.

"Perhaps our world only appears poorly designed," insists the reader. "If we understood God's designs better, that appearance would dissolve. God has no obligation to reveal all his plans to us. Is it not mere vanity to suppose that the way things appear to us is the way things really are?" No, I do not believe that it is. If God existed, then the world would be his artifact, and its superlative design would express his infinite wisdom. But one of the things we know about well-designed artifacts is that they appear well designed even to nonexperts. A Beethoven symphony, for example, sounds beautiful even to those of us who have never played an instrument. A BMW feels roomy, comfortable, and powerful even to drivers who know nothing of automotive mechanics. Similarly, a world designed by a supreme being ought to appear well designed to the ordinary mortals who live in it. No amount of explanation can turn cacophony into melody, or turn a clunker into a luxury sedan. By the same token, no future account of the world's architecture can ever explain away its evident design flaws.

5

I have argued thus far as if the fact of human freedom could be taken as granted. The reader must be wondering why I made such a presumption. Making it would appear to complicate my case against theism, while also putting my position at odds with a scientific world view. This appearance, however, is deceiving. Properly understood, human freedom is totally compatible with modern science.

The belief in freedom is one of those natural beliefs that human beings cannot shake off, no matter how hard we try. Like our belief in a mind-independent material world, it something we habitually assume in our actions, even when we doubt it in our speculations. Our skepticism, dwelling only in the study, dies as soon as we venture out into the practical affairs of life. This does not prove that our belief in freedom is true. It simply means that we may take it as the default assumption, pending evidence to the contrary.

It is sometimes thought that scientific determinism would provide that evidence. Assume, then, that determinism is true. Every event in the history of the universe is preordained, because every event follows from the universe's initial conditions, plus the operation of natural laws. Given those laws, and an exact specification of the initial conditions, every event could be predicted with certainty, provided one had the necessary computational power. Would this necessarily remove free will from the picture?

No, it would not. In every free act there is going to be a trio of elements. There will be a circle of possible actions one can do, a smaller circle inside that of actions representing live options, and finally, within that circle, rests the single action one will ultimately decide to perform. Think of that one action as being a point inside the smaller circle. By definition, freedom entails having a range of options from which to choose. The availability of multiple options is both the necessary, and a sufficient, condition of freedom. We are thus free as long as the outer circle encompasses a plurality of points. Freedom vanishes only if both circles collapse, like a black hole, into the singularity of that one point, the point representing what we will do. From the standpoint of freedom, it does not matter whether we arrive at that point through the operation of deterministic laws, or probabilistic ones. It does not matter if our action is predictable with certainty, or entirely unpredictable. All that really matters is that the point exists within a circle of options, and that the circle only collapses when we make it collapse by deciding what to do.

Determinism claims that whatever actions we perform will be predictable, given ideal conditions for making the prediction. Determinism is thus all about the one action we will perform in any given situation. It has nothing to say regarding the size of the circle within which that one action occurs. Our circle of options does not automatically collapse if our eventual action is (under obviously unrealizable conditions) predictable. It is perfectly coherent to say both "I can do a, b, c, d

…" and "I will, without any question, do z." "I can" is entirely compatible with "I won't." So even if the probability of z is 1, and the probabilities of our doing a, b, c, d … are all zero, z might for all that be a free choice. "Free" does not mean "unpredictable." Predictable does not imply "compulsory" or "forced."

"You have gotten it all wrong," the reader might object. The items a, b, c, and d all have to be possible, otherwise they are not genuine options. But how can something be possible, when the probability of it happening is zero? Isn't an event with zero probability by definition impossible?" Yes. In one perfectly natural sense of the word "possible," an event with zero probability is "impossible." However, in another, equally natural sense, a possible event is simply one that we have the power to bring about. An event may be possible in the latter sense, even when it is not in the former. We may have the power to do a thing, even if there is zero chance of our exercising that power. I have the power to quit my job, move to Tibet, and join a monastery. There is, however, zero chance of my doing that. Someone with a perfect knowledge of the world's current state of affairs could perhaps predict with certainty that I will never join a Tibetan monastery. Anyone who knows me could make the same prediction, even without such an immense fund of knowledge. It does not follow that forces beyond my control are compelling me to stay where I am. If I stay, I do so freely, but, of course, rather predictably. The notion that scientific determinism renders us powerless is just another piece of metaphysical fancy. It does not follow from the logic of the situation.

Why don't we consider this "metaphysical fancy" in more detail. Imagine being in a rail car that has been placed on a set of train tracks. The tracks prevent us from turning either left or right. We thus have no choice but to follow the tracks where they take us. Philosophers and laymen alike often speak as though determinism would put us on just such tracks. But this imagery is absurd. There are no tracks, and there would not be, even if determinism were true. Train tracks exert force on rail cars. They are (part of) the efficient cause that makes rail cars go where they go. But the laws of nature on which determinism depends exert no force on anyone. They are not real objects in the world, but only abstract patterns in the way events unfold. Natural laws are not efficient causes of natural events. They are more like the formal causes of those events. There is thus no legitimate analogy between their relation to us, and the relation train tracks have with rail cars. Natural laws cannot compel us to do anything, and thus cannot eliminate our freedom of choice.

One might argue that it is the forces of nature, not the laws of nature, which lock us onto the railroad tracks of fate. On this view, human choices are embedded within the web of natural cause and effect. But if all of our choices have causes, and if those causes operate according to deterministic laws, then true freedom of choice must be an illusion. Physical forces, perhaps combined with cultural, economic, and historical forces, conspire to produce the collapse of our circles. The confederacy of those forces compels us to act exactly as we do, and not otherwise.

The view just described depends on confusing causes with compulsions. All compulsive forces are of course also causes. But not every cause acting upon us acts with compulsive force. That our choices always have causes does not entail that we are always making them under duress.

Imagine yourself playing a game of chess. Your opponent takes your rook with his knight. His action comes as a surprise. You reexamine the board and discover that you will be mated in just three moves unless you use your remaining rook to take his bishop. So that is what you do. You take his bishop with your rook. In this situation it would be perfectly appropriate to say that your opponent's move caused yours. Had he acted differently, then your action would also have been different. Yet he did not literally force you to move the way you did, did he? You still had a choice. There were many other moves available to you. You simply chose the one move that made the most sense. In the same situation a less skilled player might not have discovered the rook takes bishop maneuver, and so would have given in to the temptation to move his queen. So when we say that your opponent's action caused yours, the causation involved here obviously does not remove you from the equation. Your intelligence, your skill, and your will to win still matter. You are still an active agent in the game, freely making choices based on your own rationally formulated strategies. Of course your action was predictable. Anyone who knew how good a chess player you are could have foreseen that you would move your rook in the right way. But the predictability of your move does not eliminate the freedom with which it was made. Accurately predicting your move would not in this case involve discerning the forces that compel you to make it. It would instead involve knowing the options available to you, and understanding how a person of your advanced skill is likely to assess each.

The situations we face in daily life are relevantly similar to this game of chess. Our choices have causes, but our freedom is not compromised by that. The forces of nature do not literally compel our every action, any more than our opponents in a chess game compel our every move. We are ourselves forces of nature. We act in the world. We are causes not just effects. Other forces have the effects on us that they do only because we choose to respond to them in certain ways. Our response is not a mere reflex, but an expression of the strategies we pursue. It is thus within our power to control that response.

If deterministic laws cannot enslave our wills by locking us onto the great railroad tracks of fate, then neither can probabilistic laws put us at the mercy of chance. It is not as though we would be like the captains of rudderless boats, set adrift in the ocean to be blown hither and yon by the winds of fortune. The rudderless boat imagery is just as absurd as the railroad metaphor, for pretty much the same reason.

This is why science cannot falsify our natural belief in freedom. Science can no more prove freedom to be an illusion, than it can prove consciousness, or the material universe, to be illusions.

Conclusion

1

We have arrived at the end of our journey. I have taken the reader as far up the ladder as I myself have gone. Although we are still deep inside the cave, we have succeeded in climbing up quite a few rungs. We may even have reached a ledge from which further progress can be made. Just think of all we have accomplished. We have learnt what truth and wisdom are. We have identified key features of the human condition. We have clarified the status of our moral beliefs. We have proven that there is no God. So here we are, we vice-ridden moral agents and foolish philosophers, all lodged together in a cave, burdened with a human nature ill designed for the task of making our escape. We do, however, possess a ladder, which is the power of our human reason, so nothing prevents us from continuing to climb our way out. Now if we could just reach that next rung …

Exasperated readers will at this point complain that my view of the world is unbearably bleak. They must think I am quite the nihilist, unable to find any meaning or value in human life. "Without God," they will say, "there is no hope, and life must be a pointless and empty march towards death." But why should an atheist have to be a nihilist? Whether our lives have meaning depends not on what propositions we believe, but on the attitudes we adopt. As the Stoic philosopher Epictetus put it in the very first line of his *Enchiridion*, "There are things which are within our power, and there are things which are beyond our power."[25] It is not within our power to fix the truth values of philosophical propositions. The structure of reality is outside our control. Yet our attitudes towards that structure belong to us. They are ours to control. So if you wish to approach life with a spiritual attitude, go ahead. Doing so does not obligate you to believe in spirits. Do you wish to love your fellow human beings, and treat them with dignity and respect? You might do that just because it is the right way to live. You do not need God's permission. Climb whatever ladders you please in life. No one is stopping you. You are free.

"And if we are not free?" I have already argued that we enjoy a certain metaphysical liberty. Suppose I am wrong about that. Even then our lives would mean a great deal to us. In fact, they would mean pretty much what they mean now. Little would change. If our lives unfold according to fate, the proposition that they do so would be just another truth for the philosopher to embrace. Such truths cannot hurt us. No truth in philosophy can. Every philosophical verity can be relished if looked at from the right perspective. Again, attitude is all. One learns to love the world the way it is. Has the reader not heard of *amor fati*?

2

The account of virtue in the first essay ended with independence. The reflections just offered suggest that a seventh virtue might be added to the list. Let us call it "fearlessness." Independence involved freedom from masters. The independent thinker has no master because he learns from so many. Fearlessness, we might say, involves freedom from propositions. The fearless thinker believes many propositions, but he is emotionally dependent on none. There is no proposition or set of propositions upon which his happiness rests. He may therefore consider the truth or falsity of any proposition objectively, without fearing the consequences if his investigation fails to produce some preferred result. His thoughts are free to go where reason leads them. The fearful thinker, on the other hand, is bound to affirm whatever propositions hold his happiness hostage. His "faith" must "seek understanding" of them. His will must coerce his intellect into accepting whatever sophistries belief in those propositions entails. But a faith infected with this kind of fear is ultimately based on a lie. No particular belief is essential to happiness. Freedom of thought begins only when one uproots this lie.

Another virtue demands another cup. This one contains no tea. The empty cup leaves room for the tea not yet brewed. It symbolizes all the insights that fearless inquiry may someday attain.

Bibliography

Ayer, Alfred Jules. 1952. *Language, Truth and Logic*. New York: Dover Publications.

Berkeley, George. 1988. *The Principles of Human Knowledge*. London: Penguin Books.

Dawkins, Richard. 1976. *The Selfish Gene*. Oxford: Oxford University Press.

———. 2006. *The God Delusion*. London: Bantam Press.

———. 2009. *The Greatest Show on Earth*. New York: Free Press.

Dennett, Daniel C. 1995. *Darwin's Dangerous Idea*. New York: Simon & Schuster.

Epictetus. 1955. *The Enchiridion*. (Trans. Thomas W. Higginson [New York: Macmillan Publishing Company].)

Flew, Antony. 1984. *God: A Critical Enquiry*. La Salle, Illinois: Open Court Publishing.

———. 1989. *An Introduction to Western Philosophy*. New York: Thames and Hudson.

Glynn, Patrick. 1997. *God: The Evidence*. Rocklin, California: Prima Publishing.

Gould, S. J. 1999. *Rocks of Ages: Science and Religion in the Fullness of Life*. New York: Ballantine.

Hume, David. 1969. "Inquiry Concerning Human Understanding," in *Ten Great Works of Philosophy* (Ed. Robert Paul Wolff [New York: Mentor].)

————. 1984. *A Treatise of Human Nature*. New York: Penguin Classics.

————. 1989. *Dialogues Concerning Natural Religion*. Buffalo: Prometheus Books.

James, William. 1907. *Pragmatism*. New York: Longmans, Green and Company.

————. 1956. *The Will to Believe and Other Essays*. New York: Dover.

Kaufmann, Walter. 1974. *Nietzsche: Philosopher, Psychologist, Antichrist*. Princeton: Princeton University Press.

Kirkham, Richard L. 1992. *Theories of Truth: A Critical Introduction*. Boston: MIT Press.

Lewis, C. S. 1943. *Mere Christianity*. New York: Collier Books, Macmillan Publishing Company.

Miller, Kenneth R. 1999. *Finding Darwin's God*. New York: HarperCollins.

Nielsen, Kai. 1990. *Ethics Without God*. Amherst, New York: Prometheus Books.

Plato. 1956. *Great Dialogues of Plato*. (Trans. W. H. D. Rouse [New York: Penguin].)

Putnam, Hilary. 1981. *Reason, Truth and History*. Cambridge: Cambridge University Press.

Schmitt, Frederick F. *Truth: A Primer*. Boulder: Westview Press.

Schopenhauer, Arthur. 1965. *On the Basis of Morality.* (Trans. E. F. J. Payne [New York: The Bobbs-Merrill Company].)

———. 1966. *The World as Will and Representation.* (Trans. E. F. J. Payne [New York: Dover].)

Steele, David Ramsay. 2008. *Atheism Explained: From Folly to Philosophy.* Chicago: Open Court.

Swinburne, Richard. 1991. *The Existence of God.* New York: Oxford University Press.

Wittgenstein, Ludwig. 1953. *Philosophical Investigations.* (Trans. G. E. M. Anscombe [New York: Macmillan Publishing Company].)

Endnotes

1. Plato's Cave Allegory is contained in Book VII of the *Republic*. For the Doctrine of Recollection, see the *Meno*.
2. Although I did not realize it at the time, my criticisms of James' pragmatism were hardly original. For a more thorough, but still brief, critical review of the pragmatic theory of truth, see chapter 3 in Frederick Schmitt's *Truth: A Primer*.
3. Nietzsche's comment is from *Will to Power*. Quotation of the relevant passage can be found in Walter Kaufmann's *Nietzsche: Philosopher, Psychologist, Antichrist*, p. 19.
4. For Hume's discussion of "is" vs. "ought," see *A Treatise of Human Nature*, Book III, Section 1. There are a couple of arguments one might offer against Hume's view. One might say, first, that the fact/value dichotomy cannot be legitimate, because many words in our language are used to both describe and evaluate. To claim that so and so committed regicide, for example, is both to describe what happened (someone killed the King) and to suggest that what they did was wrong. One might further

argue that even when not employing value laden words such as "regicide," our apparently factual statements still embody evaluative judgments. For how do we pick some facts to discuss and not others, except by applying our personal value judgments concerning what is, and is not, important? And how can we decide what the "facts" even are, except by presupposing what some philosophers call "cognitive values," such as a preference for simple theories over complex ones? Neither of these arguments is valid. As to the first, the fact that many words do two jobs in our language does not imply that there is no important difference between those jobs. The jobs are logically distinct, even though we often do them simultaneously. If so and so killed the King, an observer with monarchist sympathies might well describe that by saying "So and so committed regicide." Revolutionaries, on the other hand, might proclaim "So and so killed the King. Hooray!" Any given fact can always be re-described with a different evaluative spin, for the simple reason that facts do not fix values—precisely the point made in the main text. As for the second argument, there is a world of difference between cases where our value judgments motivate or justify our claims, and cases where value judgments constitute the claim being made. The sentence "So and so killed the King" may well embody certain evaluative judgments, yet those judgments are not what is at issue in the sentence. This has to be distinguished from the sentence "So and so committed regicide," where the speaker's evaluative stance is precisely what is at issue. The logical chasm between claims about what is the case, and claims concerning what ought to be the case, thus remains intact, even though, of course, our opinions concerning what ought to be color everything we say.

5. Hume's reflections on this subject may be found in his "Inquiry Concerning Human Understanding."

6. This formula for the correspondence theory of truth can be traced back to Aristotle's *Metaphysics*.

7. See Wittgenstein, *Philosophical Investigations*, p. 7.

8. Kierkegaard's comment on Hegel appears in Walter Kaufmann's *Nietzsche: Philosopher, Psychologist, Antichrist*, p. 85.

9. It may at first appear that I have left the concept of W_r too vague. I have not, for example, specified whether abstractions such as love and justice belong to reality. Nor have I tried to say whether reality fundamentally consists of minds, or bodies, or some combination of the two. This is by design. As I mentioned in *The Ladder*'s introduction, containment theory is not permitted any metaphysical baggage. This does not entail hostility to metaphysics; it simply means that a theory of truth should not prejudge the results of other philosophical investigations. It should instead create a level playing field on which those investigations can take place. In the debates between realists and idealists, materialists and dualists, theists and atheists, containment theory must remain neutral. I happen to be an atheist, a materialist, and a metaphysical realist. Yet my biases on these issues have no bearing on the W_r concept, as deployed by containment theory. If, for example,

it turns out that reality consists entirely of minds and their ideas, that fact would not invalidate the W_r concept. It would simply mean that I have been stupendously wrong in my opinions concerning W_r's contents. The same principle applies to the issue of abstractions. Containment theory is not at liberty to say whether love and justice "exist." It can only say that if those things do exist, if they are part of the world's furniture, then obviously they fall within the realm of W_r. My description of W_r in the main text does refer to specific items, of the sort that most people (including myself) would very naturally take to be parts of reality. These references are made purely for heuristic purposes. W_r is defined simply as the totality of things that do now, ever have, or ever will exist, together with all their actions, relations, and attributes. Containment theory has to remain agnostic concerning what exactly that totality might consist of.

10. A "multi-world," whose parts are unconnected, has to be distinguished from a "multi-verse," where multiple universes are conjoined into a single system. The universes that compose a multi-verse might be connected by wormholes or other devices. It is thus possible that our universe is just one of many universes inside a great multi-verse, and that our multi-verse is just one sub-world inside some huge mega-world.

11. Containment theory's flight from anthropocentrism is affected in part by how it defines a proposition. It defines the term "proposition" according to logical function. What binds the members of a proposition

together is a given "cut" in **B**. The cut creates a class of possible worlds, namely, the worlds that constitute the proposition's M. This logical function of cutting **B** is central to truth theory because a proposition's cut is what determines its truth value. Yet a cut is not an event in anyone's mind. So, by focusing on cuts, we are distancing truth theory from psychology. We make it a purely logical account. We could, of course, also define a "proposition" according to psychological functioning. On that view, two statements express the same proposition if and only if they employ the same concepts, and put them into the same relations with one another. A psychological account of propositions works well for describing human behavior in terms of people's beliefs and desires. It is actually the best account to give whenever our concern is to explain mental activity. For truth theory, however, concepts are simply the knives with which cuts get made. It is the cut that matters, not the composition of the knife. It would be senseless to argue over which account of propositions we ought to prefer. Each has its appropriate use, so we need both.

12. Looking at the tremendous variety of statements that fall under P^λ, one might wonder if P^λ makes an appropriate vehicle of belief. Can we be said to believe that P^λ? Yes, I think that we can. To believe that a given proposition is true is not to stand ready to affirm every one of its instances. If we accept any instance, that is enough. Consider again the statement S(1) about the Battle of Hastings. To accept that statement is to accept the proposition

it expresses. There are an indefinitely large variety of other ways to express that same proposition, and I would not accept them all, if only because many of them occur in languages I do not speak. My inability to recognize all instances of the proposition in no way compromises my belief in it. The same principle holds for P^λ. I believe it, even though my willingness to affirm it may be confined to only a tiny fraction of its instances.

13. See Daniel Dennett, *Darwin's Dangerous Idea.*

14. There is a reason for calling this a theorem in containment theory, instead of making it an axiom or definition. We cannot use the concepts of M and N to define if/then relations, because we appealed to such relations when explaining how Ms and Ns get constructed. To avoid circularity, we must define implication some other way. For example, we might say that "P implies Q" means "it is impossible to have both P and not-Q." The terms "possible" and "impossible" would then be left among the undefined terms of the system.

15. Perceptive readers may have noticed a potential contradiction. When discussing chasms earlier, I defended Hume's claim that "is" never implies "ought." But if true moral statements express P^λ, and if all truths entail P^λ, as I also claimed, then it would appear that every true statement concerning what is will entail every moral truth. Am I thus trapped in a contradiction? No. We must distinguish two senses of "entail." In one sense, every instance of P^λ entails every other instance, because the M of every instance is a subset of the M of every other instance.

In another, perfectly natural sense, however, an instance such as "2 + 2 = 4" certainly does not entail that "the sum of the angles of any triangle add up to two right angles." Both statements express P^λ, yet they do not entail one another, because they belong to different deductive-axiomatic systems. The first belongs to arithmetic, the other to Euclidean geometry. We need not choose between these two senses. Each is useful. Both serve the purpose of preserving truth values when reasoning from one claim to another. For clarity, we might call these two kinds of implication "essential implication" and "intensional implication," respectively. Hume was no doubt thinking of intensional implication, and according to that, he was right. "Is" really doesn't entail "ought." For a discussion of various types of implication, see Chapter 1 in Kirkham's *Theories of Truth*.

16. The "us" in this sentence means "non-Muslim westerners." "Them" refers to militant Muslims. Less radical Muslims are left out only because their existence presents less of a challenge to Lewis' thesis.

17. I declared earlier that a theory of truth ought not to carry any metaphysical baggage. Some readers might be concerned that by granting the reality of a moral law, I am sneaking a metaphysical postulate into containment theory. They may also worry that if we grant the reality of a moral law, then we must also grant the reality of moral facts. This would seem to eliminate the fact/value dichotomy, and hence bridge Hume's chasm between "is" and "ought."

These concerns are groundless. If the reader pleases we can of course speak of moral facts, meaning simply that there are moral truths. However, this way of speaking would not eliminate the crucial distinction between ordinary empirical facts on the one hand, and our evaluative judgments concerning those facts on the other. Hume's chasm between these two very disparate types of "fact" remains as wide as ever. Granting the reality of a moral law does nothing to bridge the chasm; it merely provides a basis for saying that statements made on both sides of that chasm can possess truth values. The moral law stands entirely on the "ought" side of the chasm. There is no "is" to it. We cannot say of the moral law that it exists. Moral laws, like logical laws, apply everywhere, but exist nowhere. Granting the reality, or in other words, the universal validity, of moral laws is thus no more "metaphysical" than granting the reality or universal validity of logic.

18. I claim in this passage that life is good, and I further take for granted that this view is not arbitrary, but is, one might say, a basic presupposition of the moral law. Many readers of philosophy will, however, think immediately of the great German pessimist Arthur Schopenhauer, who held a contrary view. Is he not a tremendous counter-example to my thesis? I do not believe so. To say that a claim is not arbitrary is not to say that it has never been controversial. Schopenhauer regarded life as bad because it inevitably involves suffering. That suffering is an evil, and hence something we ought both to avoid ourselves and also help others

avoid, is another, equally valid presupposition of morality. Schopenhauer thus rejected one aspect of the moral law in order to give what he considered due weight to another, apparently conflicting aspect. His reflections on this matter do not refute my contentions; they merely illustrate the manner in which objective elements of morality interact with more personal elements. Schopenhauer reacted to the reality of human suffering in one way; other thinkers obviously have different reactions. But these varying reactions may still be viewed as alternative interpretations of those common principles of humanity which, following Lewis, I have been calling the moral law.

19. See also Isaiah, 45:18 (Today's New International Version): "he who fashioned and made the earth, he founded it; he did not create it to be empty, but formed it to be inhabited."

20. David Ramsay Steele discusses an abbreviated version of the argument in *Atheism Explained*, only to reject it.

21. See Charles Darwin, *The Origin of Species*. For an excellent modern defense of Darwinism, written by a theist, see Kenneth Miller, *Finding Darwin's God*. For a more atheistic view of evolution by natural selection, see Richard Dawkins, *The Greatest Show on Earth*.

22. The most prominent advocate of the compatibility of science and religion might be Stephen J. Gould. For his thoughts on that subject, see *Rocks of Ages*.

23. The story of the giraffe's laryngeal nerve comes from Richard Dawkins, *The Greatest Show on Earth*, p. 360.
24. See Richard Dawkins, *The Selfish Gene*.
25. Epictetus, *The Enchiridion*, Thomas W. Higginson translation, p.17.